The Pink Salt Weight Loss Trick Plan:

A Complete Guide to Using Organic Himalayan Salt for Detox, with Morning Rituals and a Diet to Boost Well Being & Natural Health | Includes a 60-Day Meal Plan with Recipes

ELENA HARTWELL

To everyone who has chosen to care for themselves with love and intention.
May each grain of pink salt remind you of the beauty in simplicity and the power of small daily actions.
May this journey bring you health, balance, and a renewed light—inside and out.
With gratitude,
Elena Hartwell

CONTENTS

1. Avocado Toast with Poached Egg and Pink Salt – ~195 kcal
2. Greek Yogurt with Berries, Chia Seeds, and Pink Salt Granola – ~190 kcal
3. Scrambled Eggs with Spinach and Pink Salt – ~170 kcal
4. Pink Salt Banana Protein Pancakes – ~195 kca
5. Smoothie Bowl with Coconut Flakes and Pink Salt – ~180 kcal
6. Oatmeal with Almond Butter, Cinnamon, and Pink Salt – ~190 kca
7. Sweet Potato Hash with Red Onions and Pink Salt – ~180

kca

8. Cottage Cheese and Pineapple Bowl with Pink Salt – ~160 kcal
9. Zucchini and Feta Omelet with Pink Salt – ~185 kcal
10. Almond Flour Muffins with Pink Salt and Dark Chocolate Chips – ~200 kcal
11. Quinoa Salad with Chickpeas, Cucumber, Lemon, and Pink Salt – ~190 kcal
12. Watermelon, Feta, and Mint Salad with a Touch of Pink Salt – ~180 kcal
13. Arugula, Avocado, and Grapefruit Salad with Pink Salt Vinaigrette – ~200 kcal
14. Roasted Beet and Goat Cheese Salad with Pink Salt – ~200 kcal
15. Caprese Salad with Heirloom Tomatoes and Pink Salt Flakes – ~180 kcal
16. Grilled Peach and Burrata Salad with Honey and Pink Salt – ~190 kcal
17. Kale and Cranberry Salad with Lemon-Pink Salt Dressing – ~200 kcal
18. Edamame and Sesame Salad with Pink Salt – ~180 kcal
19. Lentil and Roasted Veggie Salad with Pink Salt – ~200 kcal
20. Spinach and Apple Salad with Walnut-Pink Salt Crumble – ~190 kcal
21. Carrot-Ginger Soup with Pink Salt – ~95 kcal
22. Creamy Tomato Basil Soup with Pink Salt – ~120 kcal
23. Bone Broth Enhanced with Pink Himalayan Salt – ~45 kcal
24. Lentil Soup with Cumin and Pink Salt – ~165 kcal
25. Chicken and Wild Rice Soup with Pink Salt – ~180 kcal
26. Cauliflower and Leek Soup with a Pink Salt Crunch – ~100 kcal
27. Spicy Black Bean Soup with Pink Salt – ~190 kcal
28. Butternut Squash Soup with Coconut Milk and Pink Salt – ~180 kcal
29. Miso Soup with Tofu and Pink Salt Substitute – ~90 kcal
30. Green Pea and Mint Soup with Pink Salt Garnish – ~130 kcal
31. Grilled Lemon-Herb Chicken with Pink Salt – ~190 kcal
32. Baked Salmon with Garlic, Dill, and Pink Salt – ~195 kcal
33. Stir-Fried Tofu with Vegetables and Pink Salt Soy Glaze –

~180 kcal

34. Quinoa-Stuffed Bell Peppers with Pink Salt – ~170 kcal
35. Cauliflower "Steaks" with Chimichurri and Pink Salt – ~150 kcal
36. Sweet Potato and Black Bean Tacos with Pink Salt Crema – ~195 kcal
37. Turkey Meatballs in Tomato-Pink Salt Sauce – ~180 kcal
38. Grilled Shrimp Skewers with Lime and Pink Salt – ~110 kcal
39. Moroccan Chickpea Stew with Pink Salt – ~170 kcal

40. Seared Tuna Salad Bowl with Avocado and Pink Salt – ~190 kcal
41. Baked Kale Chips with Pink Salt – ~70 kcal
42. Roasted Sweet Potato Wedges with Paprika and Pink Salt – ~130 kcal
43. Hummus with Olive Oil and Pink Salt Topping – ~160 kcal
44. Guacamole with Lime and Pink Salt – ~120 kcal
45. Cucumber and Dill Yogurt Dip with Pink Salt – ~90 kcal
46. Steamed Edamame with Crushed Pink Salt – ~120 kcal
47. Roasted Chickpeas with Garlic and Pink Salt – ~140 kcal
48. Zucchini Fritters with Pink Salt Yogurt Sauce – ~180 kcal
49. Beetroot Chips with Pink Salt – ~80 kcal
50. Baked cauliflower bites with pink salt – ~100 kca
51. Dark chocolate bark with almonds and pink salt – ~180 kcal
52. Sea Salt Caramel Energy Balls with Dates and Pink Salt - Calories per serving: ~95 kcal (1 ball)
53. Baked Apples with Cinnamon, Nuts, and Pink Salt - Calories per serving: ~160 kcal
54. Peanut Butter–Pink Salt Fudge - Calories per serving: ~100 kcal (1 piece)
55. Almond–Pink Salt Granola Bars - Calories per serving: ~190 kcal (1 bar)
56. Coconut Macaroons with a Hint of Pink Salt - Calories per serving: ~95 kcal (1 macaroon)
57. Pink Salt Chocolate Avocado Mousse - Calories per serving: ~180 kcal
58. Oatmeal Cookies with Pink Salt Flakes - Calories per serving: ~95 kcal (1 cookie)

Writing this book has been a journey of research, passion, and deep respect for the natural wisdom that has supported human well-being for centuries. First and foremost, I want to thank those who believed in this project from the beginning and encouraged the idea of sharing a simple, sustainable, and mindful approach to wellness through the use of Himalayan pink salt.

A special thank-you goes to the nutritionists, herbalists, and wellness professionals who inspired me with their knowledge, experiences, and guidance. Without their contributions and dedication to natural health, this book would not have had the same depth.

I am deeply grateful to my family and friends for their constant support, patience, and unconditional love throughout the writing process.

Finally, thank you to you, the reader, for choosing this book as a companion on your wellness journey. May the following pages provide you with practical tools, daily inspiration, and a deeper connection to your body and your health.

With gratitude

1. INTRODUCTION TO PINK SALT AND ITS ORIGINS

Salt is one of the oldest substances used by humans. Always present on our tables, in spiritual rituals, and in traditional medical treatments, it has taken many forms over time. But not all salt is created equal. In recent years, one type in particular has captured the attention of the health and wellness world: pink salt.

When people talk about pink salt, they often refer specifically to Himalayan pink salt, but there are actually several varieties of naturally colored salts that share similar nutritional and visual qualities. What sets pink salt apart, first and foremost, is its unique hue—ranging from pale pink to deep red—primarily due to its rich mineral and trace element content.

The most well-known is Himalayan pink salt, mined in the Khewra Salt Mine in Pakistan's Punjab region, at the foothills of the Himalayas. This ancient salt deposit was formed millions of years ago and has remained protected from modern pollution and contaminants. Even today, it is extracted using traditional methods that preserve its natural crystal structure and purity. What makes this salt truly unique, beyond its color, is its composition of over 80 trace minerals—including iron, magnesium, calcium, and potassium.

Lesser known, but equally intriguing, is Bolivian pink salt, mined in the Andes. This salt also has ancient origins and is considered a natural and uncontaminated source. While similar in composition and appearance to Himalayan salt, Bolivian pink salt is slightly less crystalline and is often appreciated for its mild taste and less intense flavor. Both varieties are used

1

not only in cooking, but also in spa treatments, skincare products, and purification rituals.

The fascination with pink salt comes not only from its aesthetics or popularity but from the combination of its history, natural origins, and functionality. In many cultures, salt has always been considered sacred—a symbol of purity, protection, and healing. Today, as people move away from heavily processed and industrialized products, there is a growing interest in more natural, less refined alternatives. In this context, pink salt is seen as a return to the roots, a more authentic and mindful way of nourishing the body and caring for oneself.

Despite growing enthusiasm, it's important to keep a realistic perspective. Pink salt, while richer in minerals than common table salt, is not a significant source of nutrients. However, its purity and the absence of chemical additives make it an appealing choice for those seeking a more natural alternative to refined salt. Its slightly milder and more complex taste can also encourage reduced salt use in meals, which may help lower overall sodium intake.

Throughout this book, we will explore how to integrate pink salt into daily diets, morning rituals, and most importantly, into a structured eating plan designed to promote general wellness and support weight loss.

2 THE SCIENCE BEHIND PINK SALT: NUTRIENTS AND BENEFITS

2.1 A NUTRITIONAL PROFILE BEYOND SODIUM

When we think of salt, we typically imagine a white, fine powder with one primary component: sodium chloride. This standard table salt has been refined, bleached, and stripped of nearly all trace minerals in the process of mass production. In contrast, pink salt—particularly Himalayan pink salt—offers something far more complex and potentially beneficial: a rich spectrum of natural minerals.

One of the key differences lies in the presence of up to 84 trace elements found in pink salt. These include iron, calcium, magnesium, potassium, zinc, and phosphorus—each essential to bodily functions, even in minute amounts. Iron, for example, not only contributes to the salt's pink to reddish hues but plays a vital role in oxygen transport in the blood. Magnesium supports nerve function and muscle health, while potassium helps regulate blood pressure and fluid balance.

Although the actual quantity of these minerals in a daily serving of pink salt is relatively small, their natural presence—in contrast to the artificial additives of table salt—makes pink salt more than just a seasoning. It becomes a mineral-rich supplement to your diet, especially when consumed as part of a balanced lifestyle.

Furthermore, the crystals of pink salt are typically larger and less processed, which means you often use less by volume compared to finely ground table salt. As a result, you get not only a broader range of minerals but also a reduction in overall sodium intake—something especially important for those managing hypertension or cardiovascular health.

In essence, pink salt shifts the concept of salt from a simple flavor enhancer to a functional food component—something that contributes, in a small but meaningful way, to your daily nutritional needs.

2.2 SUPPORTING NATURAL DETOXIFICATION PROCESS

Detoxification is a term that's often misunderstood. Despite what popular health trends might suggest, no single food or ingredient can "cleanse" your body in isolation. True detoxification is the job of your body's internal systems—especially the liver, kidneys, lungs, and skin—which work continuously to eliminate waste and toxins. However, certain nutrients can support these organs and enhance their function. This is where pink salt enters the picture.

Unlike highly processed table salt, pink salt retains a natural array of trace minerals that can contribute to the optimal functioning of detox pathways. Minerals like magnesium, potassium, and calcium help regulate cellular processes, maintain hydration, and support the body's ability to flush out waste through urine, sweat, and digestion.

One traditional method that has gained popularity is the preparation of "sole water"—a concentrated solution made by saturating water with pink salt. This tonic is often consumed first thing in the morning to promote hydration and aid electrolyte balance. While scientific research on sole water is limited, many people report feeling more energetic and experiencing improved digestion and less bloating after incorporating it into their routine.

Another important aspect is the absence of additives. Table salt typically contains anti-caking agents, synthetic iodine, and other chemical additives that some argue may burden the body over time. In contrast, pink salt is minimally processed, free from artificial compounds, and closer to its natural state.

By choosing pink salt over conventional salt, you're not introducing anything "detoxifying" in the miraculous sense, but rather supporting the body's own detox mechanisms by ensuring proper mineral intake and reducing unnecessary additives. When paired with adequate hydration, a healthy diet, and lifestyle habits like movement and rest, pink salt becomes a valuable ally in maintaining the body's natural balance and waste elimination.

2.3 BALANCING THE BODY'S pH LEVELS

The concept of "pH balance" is central to many wellness philosophies, often tied to claims that an overly acidic body leads to illness, fatigue, and inflammation. While the human body naturally regulates pH through highly controlled biological systems—especially in the blood and organs—some dietary and lifestyle choices can support this balance more effectively than others. Pink salt is frequently cited as one such supportive element.

Though pink salt is technically a mineral-rich sodium chloride, its trace elements are believed to contribute to a more alkalizing effect in the body when compared to refined white salt. Minerals such as magnesium, calcium, and potassium are known to help neutralize excess acidity, especially when consumed as part of a balanced, plant-forward diet.

In contrast, processed foods high in refined sugar, artificial additives, and preservatives—often accompanied by regular table salt—may shift the internal environment toward mild acidosis over time. While the body will always work to maintain a stable blood pH (typically around 7.35–7.45), chronic dietary stressors can place a heavier burden on organs like the kidneys and lungs, which regulate acid-base levels.

Pink salt, due to its natural composition and lack of chemical additives, can be a small but meaningful part of an alkalizing dietary approach. Its use in morning water rituals, cooking, or seasoning contributes not only to flavor but also to mineral support, helping the body maintain equilibrium.

It's also important to note that hydration plays a key role in pH regulation. Pink salt, when paired with water in proper amounts, supports electrolyte balance, which influences how effectively cells absorb nutrients and expel waste. Together, these effects contribute to a more stable internal environment—one where energy is optimized, inflammation is reduced, and wellness is sustained.

2.4 WHY PINK SALT HAS LESS SODIUM THAN TABLE SALT

One of the most commonly cited advantages of pink salt is that it contains less sodium per serving than regular table salt. At first glance, this might seem counterintuitive—after all, both are primarily composed of sodium chloride. So how can one type of salt have less sodium than another? The answer lies in the crystal structure, mineral content, and processing methods.

Pink salt, particularly Himalayan pink salt, is typically sold in larger, coarser grains. These crystals take up more space per unit of weight, meaning that when you sprinkle a teaspoon of pink salt, you're likely getting fewer sodium molecules than you would from a tightly packed teaspoon of finely ground table salt. In practical terms, this leads to a lower sodium intake per pinch, especially when pink salt is used in moderation.

Moreover, unlike table salt—which is refined to contain nearly 100% pure sodium chloride—pink salt retains a natural mix of trace minerals that slightly dilute the sodium content. While the difference isn't dramatic on a chemical level, it becomes significant in daily consumption patterns. The inclusion of minerals such as potassium, magnesium, and calcium means that pink salt is less concentrated in sodium and potentially better balanced in terms of mineral intake.

Another critical aspect is how pink salt is used. Because of its stronger, more complex flavor, many people find they use less of it overall to achieve the same taste enhancement. This naturally leads to lower sodium consumption without feeling deprived of flavor—an important consideration for those managing conditions like high blood pressure or cardiovascular disease.

Finally, pink salt contains no anti-caking agents or preservatives, which are common in table salt. These additives do not add sodium per se, but they may have other long-term health implications when consumed regularly. By choosing a more natural product like pink salt, you're avoiding these extras and consuming salt in a form that's closer to its original, mineral-rich state.

2.5 ADDITIONAL BENEFITS OF PINK SALT IN EVERYDAY HEALT

Beyond its primary functions in cooking and detox, pink salt is often praised for its potential benefits in supporting various aspects of everyday health. While the research on some of these claims may still be evolving, many people report feeling better and more balanced when they incorporate pink salt into their daily routines.

One notable benefit is improved hydration. Hydration isn't just about drinking water; it's also about ensuring that the body's cells are able to absorb and retain that water effectively. Pink salt, with its natural mineral content, helps maintain electrolyte balance, particularly sodium, potassium, and magnesium. These minerals are crucial in regulating fluid balance in and out of cells. This means that when you drink water with a pinch of pink salt (for example, in the form of sole water or a light saline solution), your body may retain moisture better and be able to transport it to the cells where it's needed most, preventing dehydration, especially in hot climates or after exercise.

Pink salt is also believed to promote healthy digestion. When consumed in small amounts, the minerals in pink salt can assist in stimulating digestive enzymes, which help break down food and facilitate the absorption of nutrients. The presence of magnesium in particular may support smooth muscle function in the intestines, aiding digestion and helping to prevent constipation. Some people even use pink salt as part of a gentle morning ritual to support bowel movements and prevent sluggish digestion.

Another often mentioned benefit is improved sleep quality. Many individuals report better sleep after using pink salt in their daily routine. This could be linked to the presence of magnesium, which plays a significant role in promoting relaxation and reducing stress. Magnesium is known to help regulate the body's production of melatonin, the hormone responsible for the sleep-wake cycle, as well as promote muscle relaxation, making it easier to unwind before bed.

Furthermore, pink salt is sometimes used for skin health. Salt baths, for instance, are an ancient remedy for soothing irritated skin, reducing inflammation, and promoting healing. The minerals in pink salt are thought to support skin regeneration and help treat conditions like eczema or psoriasis by reducing itching and dryness. While the exact mechanism is still a topic of research, many users find that bathing with pink salt or applying a salt scrub can leave their skin feeling soft and nourished.

Finally, pink salt has been suggested as a natural air purifier when used in the form of salt lamps. The theory is that as the salt lamp heats up, it attracts moisture from the air, trapping dust and allergens. While the science behind this claim is still debated, many users enjoy the calming ambiance created by these lamps and believe that they help reduce indoor pollutants. The negative ions released by salt lamps are also thought to counteract the effects of electronic pollution from devices like computers and phones, creating a more relaxed environment.

While more research is needed to confirm the extent of some of these claims, there's no doubt that the natural properties of pink salt offer a wide range of potential everyday health benefits. Whether it's improving hydration, supporting digestion, aiding relaxation, or benefiting the skin, incorporating pink salt into your routine may enhance your overall well-being in a simple, natural way.

3 WHY PINK SALT FOR WEIGHT LOSS?

The connection between pink Himalayan salt and weight loss might seem surprising at first. After all, when we think about losing weight, we usually focus on calorie counting, exercise, and avoiding salty foods. Yet, pink salt offers a different perspective—one rooted in natural wellness and the idea of supporting the body's systems rather than simply restricting it.

Unlike ordinary table salt, pink Himalayan salt is unrefined and packed with trace minerals that can benefit the body in subtle but meaningful ways. These minerals—like magnesium, potassium, and calcium—play a quiet but crucial role in helping the body maintain a healthy balance of fluids and electrolytes. This balance is essential not just for hydration but for ensuring that the body doesn't hold onto excess water, which often leads to that uncomfortable feeling of bloating many people confuse with fat gain.

Another reason pink salt is often linked to weight loss has to do with digestion. A small amount of pink salt, especially when taken with warm water or before meals, may stimulate the production of stomach acid. This helps the digestive system break down food more efficiently and absorb nutrients better. A well-functioning digestive system is vital when trying to lose weight, as poor digestion can trigger cravings, slow metabolism, and encourage the body to store more fat than it needs to.

There's also an interesting connection between pink salt and appetite control. Some people find that when they include pink salt in their meals— or sip water infused with a pinch of it—they feel more satisfied and experience fewer sugar cravings throughout the day. This could be due to its role in helping regulate blood sugar levels, which in turn affects hunger and energy. Stable energy means fewer highs and lows, fewer trips to the snack cupboard, and a more consistent eating rhythm overall.

Beyond these internal benefits, pink salt is often used in detox routines designed to help the body shed toxins and reduce inflammation. Whether it's in a saltwater flush, a morning ritual with warm lemon water and pink salt, or a relaxing mineral bath, this ancient crystal seems to support the body's natural cleansing processes. And a body that's less burdened by toxins tends to function more efficiently—including when it comes to burning fat and managing weight.

There's also a lesser-known but important angle: the impact of stress. Modern life is full of stressors that can throw our hormones—especially cortisol—out of balance. This hormonal disruption can lead to stubborn weight gain, particularly around the midsection. The trace minerals in pink salt may help support adrenal health and stabilize stress-related hormone levels, which is why many people report feeling calmer and more energized when they use it regularly.

So, is pink salt a miracle weight-loss cure? Not exactly. But it's also not just hype. When used mindfully, as part of a broader healthy lifestyle, pink Himalayan salt can support many of the body's natural systems that play a role in maintaining a healthy weight. It's not about doing less—it's about doing things smarter, and letting the body work the way it was meant to.

4 DAILY DETOX WITH PINK SALT: MORNING RITUALS AND ROUTINES

How we begin our day sets the tone for everything that follows. For those seeking natural ways to support their body's detox processes and kickstart weight loss or simply feel more energized, pink Himalayan salt has found its place as a simple but powerful morning ally.

Each morning offers a fresh start—not just mentally, but physically. While we sleep, the body works hard to repair cells, regulate hormones, and process toxins. When we wake up, it's the perfect time to assist the body in flushing out what it no longer needs. This is where pink salt can play a gentle but effective role in your daily detox routine.

One of the most popular morning practices is drinking warm water with a pinch of pink Himalayan salt—often referred to as "sole water." This ritual, ideally done on an empty stomach, helps rehydrate the body after several hours without fluids, but it does more than just quench thirst. The natural minerals in pink salt help activate the digestive system, stimulate metabolism, and encourage the gentle release of toxins that have built up overnight. People who adopt this habit often report better digestion, reduced bloating, and a clearer sense of focus in the early hours.

This warm salted water can also help regulate bowel movements, especially for those who struggle with sluggish digestion or constipation. When your digestive tract is working efficiently, the body is better equipped to eliminate waste and absorb nutrients—two fundamental elements for both detox and sustainable weight loss.

Another benefit of beginning the day with a pink salt ritual is its impact on adrenal and hormonal health. The morning is when cortisol, the body's stress hormone, naturally spikes to wake us up. But in many people, especially those under chronic stress, cortisol levels can be either too high or too low—

11

leading to fatigue, irritability, and even weight gain. The trace minerals in pink salt offer a natural way to support the adrenal glands, helping bring hormones into balance and setting a calmer, more stable tone for the day.

Some also like to combine their morning pink salt drink with fresh lemon juice. The lemon adds vitamin C and enhances the detoxifying effect, helping the liver do its job more effectively. This simple combination—just warm water, a squeeze of lemon, and a pinch of pink salt—can become a mindful morning ritual, one that nourishes both body and mind.

Beyond the internal, there are also external ways to incorporate pink salt into a detox routine. A morning bath with pink salt crystals can soothe tired muscles, improve circulation, and draw impurities from the skin. Even if it's just once or twice a week, this kind of mineral soak is a quiet yet powerful act of self-care.

The goal of a pink salt morning routine isn't to shock the system or promise dramatic overnight results. Instead, it's about supporting the body's natural rhythms and offering it the minerals, hydration, and calm start it needs to function optimally. Over time, these small choices become habits—and habits become lifestyle.

So, if you're looking for a clean, consistent way to feel lighter, clearer, and more in tune with your body, consider letting pink salt be part of your morning. One glass, one breath, one moment of intention—this is where real transformation   begins.

5 THE PINK SALT TRICK

5.1 – WHAT EXACTLY IS THE "PINK SALT TRICK"?

The "Pink Salt Trick" is a simple yet powerful method that leverages the natural properties of Himalayan pink salt to stimulate weight loss, enhance detoxification, and support overall wellness. At its core, the trick involves consuming a small amount of pink salt—often dissolved in water—at strategic times during the day to activate specific physiological responses in the body.

But why pink salt, and what makes it so special?

Unlike regular table salt, Himalayan pink salt is unrefined and contains over 80 trace minerals, including magnesium, potassium, calcium, and iron. These minerals not only give the salt its characteristic rosy hue but also contribute to vital bodily functions such as hydration, muscle contractions, nerve signaling, and pH balance.

The "trick" lies in using this mineral-rich salt as a catalyst for hydration and metabolic activation. When pink salt is dissolved in warm water—creating what's commonly referred to as **"sole water"**—it forms a mineral infusion that, when consumed first thing in the morning or before meals, can:

- **Kickstart digestion** by stimulating the production of digestive enzymes and stomach acid
- **Balance electrolytes**, supporting better energy levels and mental clarity
- **Trigger a mild detox response** by helping the body release retained water and flush out toxins
- **Curb cravings** by naturally regulating hunger and promoting satiety

This practice is not a magic pill, but rather a natural, low-effort enhancement to your daily routine that aligns with how the body functions. It supports the body's natural rhythms and detoxification pathways without introducing artificial substances or extreme dietary restrictions.

The Pink Salt Trick is often considered the "gateway" habit in the broader Pink Salt Weight Loss Plan. It's easy to implement, affordable, and—most importantly—backed by both traditional wisdom and emerging nutritional science.

5.2 – THE RIGHT TIMING: WHEN TO TAKE PINK SALT TO MAXIMIZE RESULTS

When it comes to health and weight loss, *what* you consume is important—but *when* you consume it can be just as crucial. The Pink Salt Trick is no exception. While Himalayan pink salt offers a host of benefits on its own, its effects can be significantly amplified when taken at the right moments in your daily routine.

Let's explore how proper timing can turn this simple trick into a powerful wellness ritual.

Start Your Day with a Reset: Morning Intake

One of the most effective times to use pink salt is first thing in the morning, on an empty stomach. After a long night of sleep, your body is naturally in a detox mode. Your organs have been at work repairing, cleansing, and restoring balance. What you do in the first hour after waking can either support or disrupt that process.

A glass of warm water mixed with a pinch of Himalayan pink salt acts as a gentle yet potent way to rehydrate, replenish essential minerals, and stimulate digestion. Many people report feeling more energized, lighter, and mentally clear just minutes after drinking it.

Think of it as "flipping the switch" for your metabolism—signaling your body that it's time to wake up, digest, and burn energy.

Before Meals: Prime Your Digestion

Taking pink salt water 15 to 30 minutes before a meal can prepare your digestive system for what's to come. Especially if you tend to feel bloated, sluggish, or overly full after eating, this simple step may make a big difference.

Here's why: Himalayan pink salt can increase the production of hydrochloric acid in your stomach. This acid is essential for breaking down food, absorbing nutrients, and preventing indigestion. Without enough of

it, your body struggles to process even healthy meals.
Adding this ritual before lunch or dinner is a subtle but effective way to support better digestion and long-term metabolic health.

Pre-Workout: Natural Electrolyte Support
If you're about to move your body—whether it's yoga, a brisk walk, or a gym session—consider using the Pink Salt Trick as a pre-workout hydration booster. Our muscles rely on minerals like sodium, potassium, and magnesium to contract and recover. Pink salt provides all of these in a natural, unprocessed form.
Simply add a pinch of pink salt to your water bottle and sip it 15–20 minutes before exercise. Many people find they sweat more efficiently, experience fewer cramps, and recover faster afterward.
You can also add a squeeze of lemon for added vitamin C and flavor.

After Sweating: Replenish and Rebalance
Whether it's from exercise, hot weather, or even a sauna session, sweating causes your body to lose not just water, but also key minerals. Replacing those lost electrolytes quickly is essential if you want to avoid fatigue, dizziness, or brain fog.
Instead of reaching for artificial sports drinks loaded with sugar, pink salt water offers a clean, effective alternative. It restores balance without the crash.

Before Bed: A Calming Mineral Infusion (Use with Caution)
While it might sound counterintuitive, some people find that taking a small amount of pink salt in warm water before bed actually helps them sleep better. The minerals in the salt can help regulate cortisol levels—the stress hormone that often interferes with deep, restful sleep.
This isn't for everyone, especially those with high blood pressure or salt sensitivity. But if you struggle with nighttime restlessness or wake up frequently, it might be worth experimenting with under medical guidance.

Listen to Your Body
The beauty of the Pink Salt Trick is its flexibility. You don't have to follow a rigid schedule or use it multiple times a day. In fact, starting with just *one* moment—like your morning glass—is often enough to begin feeling noticeable changes.
As you tune in to your body's responses, you'll begin to sense what works best for you. Whether it's a kickstart to your morning, a digestive aid before meals, or a hydration tool during workouts, the timing can transform this ancient mineral into a modern wellness ally.

5.3 – THE MIRACLE MIX: PINK SALT AND WARM WATER

Of all the ways to use Himalayan pink salt, there's one that stands out for its simplicity, effectiveness, and versatility: **the mix of pink salt and warm water**, often referred to as *sole water* (pronounced "so-lay"). This unassuming combination may look like nothing more than slightly cloudy water, but inside that glass is a potent, mineral-rich solution that can nourish, cleanse, and energize your body—starting from the very first sip. Let's take a deeper look at why this mix is so powerful, and how to prepare and use it correctly.

Why Warm Water? The Role of Temperature

Warm water plays a surprisingly important role in the effectiveness of the Pink Salt Trick. When you drink something warm—especially on an empty stomach—your body receives it more gently and absorbs it more easily than cold or room-temperature water. Warm water also helps stimulate digestion, wake up the liver, and activate intestinal movement, which is essential if you're aiming to detox and lose weight.

Combined with Himalayan pink salt, this becomes a *morning elixir* that both hydrates and signals your metabolism to get to work.

What Exactly Is Sole Water?

Sole water is a saturated solution made by dissolving Himalayan pink salt in water until no more salt can dissolve. What remains is a mineral-charged tonic that your body can easily assimilate. The trace minerals in pink salt—magnesium, calcium, potassium, and over 80 others—help balance your body's pH, support adrenal function, and regulate hydration at a cellular level.

You don't drink the whole jar of sole water—you just add **a teaspoon of it** to a glass of warm water when you're ready to consume it.

How to Make Sole Water (Step-by-Step Guide)
Ingredients:

* A clean glass jar with a non-metallic lid (metal can react with the salt)
* High-quality Himalayan pink salt (fine or coarse)
* Filtered water

Instructions:

1. Fill the jar about ¼ of the way with pink salt.
2. Add filtered water to the top.
3. Seal the jar and let it sit overnight.

4. By morning, if some salt is still undissolved at the bottom, your solution is ready. This means the water has become fully saturated.
5. Store it at room temperature. It doesn't go bad.

To use it: Each morning, mix 1 teaspoon of sole water into a glass of warm water. Stir, sip slowly, and wait about 20–30 minutes before eating or drinking anything else.

What You Might Feel After Drinking It
While every body is different, here are some common responses people notice after regularly drinking pink salt water:
- A gentle bowel movement shortly after
- Increased energy and focus during the morning
- Fewer cravings for sugar or snacks throughout the day
- Better hydration and less bloating
- A general feeling of being "lighter" and more balanced

These effects may not all happen overnight—but consistency makes a difference. For many, this becomes a ritual they look forward to each morning, a moment of mindfulness and self-care that sets the tone for the rest of the day.

Can You Just Mix Salt in Water Without Making Sole?
Yes—if you're short on time, you can simply stir about ¼ **to** ½ **teaspoon** of pink salt into a warm glass of water and drink it directly. It's not quite the same as sole water (which is a more mineral-rich solution), but it still offers benefits, especially when used as part of your morning ritual or pre-meal routine.

The pink salt and warm water mix is simple, safe, and surprisingly effective. You're not taking pills, powders, or processed supplements—just real, raw earth minerals in a form your body understands. When practiced consistently, this daily habit can lead to real, tangible changes in your energy, digestion, and overall well-being.

5.4 – COMMON MISTAKES TO AVOID WITH THE PINK SALT TRICK

Like many natural wellness habits, the Pink Salt Trick is simple—but not foolproof. While it may seem as easy as mixing salt and water, the *how, when,* and *how much* matter more than most people think. Misusing pink salt can not only reduce its benefits but, in some cases, actually cause discomfort or health setbacks.

Let's explore the most common mistakes people make with the Pink Salt Trick—and how to avoid them.

Mistake #1: Using Too Much Salt

More salt doesn't mean more benefits. One of the most frequent errors is thinking that a larger amount of pink salt will enhance detox or speed up weight loss. In reality, overdoing it can lead to bloating, dehydration, or even increased blood pressure in sensitive individuals.

The fix:

Stick to the recommended dose—usually ¼ to ½ teaspoon in warm water or 1 teaspoon of sole water in the morning. Let your body guide you. If you ever feel puffy, thirsty, or uncomfortable afterward, scale back.

Mistake #2: Not Drinking Enough Water Throughout the Day

Pink salt helps balance fluids and supports hydration, but only if you're actually drinking enough water. Some people mistakenly rely solely on their morning salt drink, assuming it's enough to keep them hydrated.

The fix:

Use the Pink Salt Trick as a *starting point*, not a substitute. Continue to drink water regularly throughout the day—ideally 6–8 glasses or more, depending on your activity level.

Mistake #3: Using the Wrong Type of Salt

Not all "pink salt" on the market is authentic Himalayan salt. Some products are dyed or processed, stripped of their mineral content, or mixed with fillers.

The fix:

Choose **genuine, food-grade Himalayan pink salt**, preferably from trusted sources. Look for unrefined, additive-free versions in coarse or fine form. Avoid pink salts that look unusually bright or come in generic packaging with no origin listed.

Mistake #4: Taking It at the Wrong Time

Timing is everything. Drinking pink salt water right before a heavy meal or late at night can lead to digestive discomfort or even disturb your sleep.

The fix:

The best time to take it is first thing in the morning on an empty stomach, or 15–30 minutes before a meal. Avoid taking it right before bed unless it's for a specific, calming purpose (and in a very small amount).

18

Mistake #5: Expecting Overnight Results

Many people try the Pink Salt Trick for a day or two and give up because they don't instantly feel lighter or lose weight. But like most natural habits, this trick works best with **consistency**, not intensity.

The fix:

Think of it as a long-term ally—not a crash solution. Use it daily for at least **1–2 weeks** before evaluating your results. Pair it with good nutrition, movement, and sleep for best outcomes.

A Gentle Practice, Not a Quick Fix

The Pink Salt Trick is a supportive tool, not a miracle cure. If used mindfully, it can become a quiet but powerful part of your daily rhythm. By avoiding these common mistakes, you allow the natural properties of Himalayan salt to work with your body—not against it.

Take your time, listen to your body, and allow the benefits to unfold gradually. Your health journey deserves that kind of patience and presence.

5.5 – STAYING ON TRACK: HOW TO USE THE PINK SALT TRICK ON BUSY OR OFF DAYS

Let's face it—no one lives in a perfect routine all the time. Some mornings are rushed, travel disrupts healthy habits, and stressful days can lead us straight back to sugary snacks or skipped meals. But one of the greatest strengths of the Pink Salt Trick is its *adaptability*. Unlike complex diets or supplements that require rigid schedules, pink salt is something you can return to—even on your most chaotic days.

This section will guide you on how to stay connected to the Pink Salt Trick when life gets messy.

When You Wake Up Late or Skip Breakfast

Ideally, pink salt water is taken first thing in the morning on an empty stomach. But what if you oversleep, or have to rush out the door without breakfast?

Quick tip:

Keep a small jar of sole water or a pinch of pink salt in a travel container. Mix it with warm (or even room-temperature) water as soon as you can— *even mid-morning is better than nothing.* The benefits will still activate your digestion and help balance hydration.

During Travel or Vacations

19

Airplanes, hotel food, irregular meal times—travel is the enemy of wellness routines. But pink salt can actually be your ally in these situations. Its mineral content helps fight bloating, water retention (especially from salty airplane food), and jet lag fatigue.

Travel trick:
Pack a small bag of high-quality Himalayan pink salt in your luggage. Mix it with bottled water or warm hotel tea water in the morning. Many travelers report feeling more grounded, energized, and less puffy when using pink salt abroad.

When You're Sick or Feeling Run Down
During illness or periods of low energy, your body craves minerals to support recovery—but you might not have the appetite for heavy foods or supplements. Pink salt in warm water can offer gentle nourishment and hydration when you're under the weather.
Bonus:
You can add a little raw honey and lemon to make a comforting immune-boosting drink.

After Overeating or "Cheat Days"
We all have those days—celebrations, holidays, emotional eating. The key is not punishment, but *rebalancing*. Pink salt water the next morning can help reset digestion, reduce water retention, and prevent the urge to spiral into more poor choices.
Mindset shift:
Instead of guilt, let your morning salt drink become a signal: *I'm back on track. My body is still my priority.*

On Mentally Exhausting Days
Not every "off" day is physical—some are emotional. Stress, anxiety, brain fog, or low mood can make even basic self-care feel hard. Surprisingly, this is where rituals like the Pink Salt Trick can help the most.
The act of preparing your drink, taking a few mindful sips, and giving your body something *pure* and nourishing can re-center your day in a quiet, powerful way.

Flexibility Makes It Sustainable
The Pink Salt Trick isn't about perfection—it's about *connection*. A small, grounding habit that can travel with you, adjust to your life, and remind your body that wellness is still within reach.
Even on the messiest days, a simple glass of warm pink salt water can be your reset button.

6 BUILDING A SUSTAINABLE PINK SALT DIET: WHAT TO EAT AND AVOID

Embarking on a wellness journey with pink Himalayan salt as a supporting element doesn't mean transforming your diet overnight or adopting extreme restrictions. Instead, it's about building a sustainable, nourishing way of eating that aligns with your body's natural rhythms—and using pink salt to enhance, not dominate, that process.

The idea behind a "pink salt diet" isn't that you consume large amounts of salt. Quite the opposite: it's about replacing heavily processed table salt, which has been stripped of its natural minerals and often contains additives, with a more wholesome, mineral-rich alternative. Pink salt becomes a tool for balance—helping regulate hydration, support digestion, and bring flavor to meals without burdening the body.

A sustainable pink salt diet starts with real, whole foods. Think vibrant vegetables, leafy greens, whole grains like quinoa and brown rice, legumes, nuts, seeds, and high-quality proteins like wild-caught fish, organic chicken, or eggs. These foods provide the body with nutrients that work in harmony with the minerals found in pink salt, allowing your metabolism, digestion, and detox pathways to work smoothly and efficiently.

When preparing these meals, pink salt can be used mindfully to season and enhance flavor without overwhelming the dish. Its more complex, earthy taste often means you need less of it compared to conventional salt. It also encourages slower, more conscious eating—something that in itself supports digestion and weight regulation.

What should you avoid? The main focus is steering clear of highly processed and packaged foods. These often contain high levels of sodium in the form of refined salt, preservatives, and artificial flavorings that disrupt the body's mineral balance and contribute to bloating, inflammation, and water retention. Sugary snacks, refined carbs like white bread and pasta, and deep-fried foods can also work against your goals, making it harder for your body to absorb nutrients and flush toxins.

Equally important is paying attention to how you eat, not just what you eat. A sustainable pink salt lifestyle encourages rituals around food: cooking at home when possible, eating slowly, and staying well-hydrated throughout the day. Drinking water with a small pinch of pink salt, especially in the morning or after sweating, helps maintain electrolyte balance and supports energy levels.

For snacks, options like raw veggies with hummus, boiled eggs with a sprinkle of pink salt and paprika, or avocado on seeded crackers can satisfy cravings while keeping your nutrient intake high and your salt levels clean. Even sweet treats can be adapted—dark chocolate with a hint of pink salt, or fruit with a light salted nut butter, offer both pleasure and balance.

It's not about perfection. It's about progress, consistency, and finding joy in nourishing your body without harsh rules. A sustainable pink salt diet is flexible, flavorful, and grounded in nature. It honors your health without demanding sacrifice—and in that, it becomes something you can carry with you long after any 30-day challenge or detox plan ends.

By choosing foods that support your well-being and seasoning them with intention, you're not just changing what's on your plate. You're building a lifestyle that respects your body, your goals, and the rhythms of real life.

7 PHYSICAL AND MENTAL BENEFITS BEYOND WEIGHT LOSS

While many are drawn to pink Himalayan salt for its potential role in weight loss, its real value stretches far beyond the scale. In fact, focusing solely on weight can sometimes obscure the deeper, more lasting transformations that occur when we nourish the body with intention. Pink salt, in its pure and natural form, offers a wide array of benefits that impact physical vitality, mental clarity, and overall well-being.

Let's begin with the body. One of the most immediate effects of replacing processed salt with pink Himalayan salt is improved hydration. Pink salt contains essential trace minerals—such as magnesium, potassium, and calcium—that help the body retain and balance fluids more effectively. This isn't just about avoiding dehydration; it's about supporting cellular health. When your cells are properly hydrated and mineralized, they function more efficiently, leading to better energy, improved muscle performance, and a greater sense of physical resilience throughout the day.

This mineral support can also lead to fewer muscle cramps, especially for those who are physically active or prone to electrolyte imbalances. After exercise or sweating, a pinch of pink salt in water can help replenish what the body has lost, allowing for quicker recovery and less fatigue. And for people who suffer from chronic inflammation, pink salt's natural anti-inflammatory properties—alongside a clean, whole-food diet—can gently support the body in calming down systemic irritation and stiffness.

Beyond the physical, pink salt can also positively influence the nervous system. Minerals like magnesium are known to calm the mind and support deeper, more restful sleep. Many people who introduce pink salt into their evening routine—perhaps in a warm bath, or with a mineral-rich broth—find that they sleep more soundly and wake up feeling more refreshed. This improved rest can have ripple effects: better mood regulation, more stable energy, and sharper mental focus.

The mental benefits of pink salt go even further when we consider its effect on stress. Today's fast-paced lifestyle often leaves the nervous system overloaded, which in turn disrupts hormonal balance and emotional stability. Pink salt, when taken mindfully and in moderation, can help regulate the adrenal glands—the body's stress managers—by providing the minerals needed to balance cortisol levels and reduce the feeling of being "wired but tired." This creates a more grounded, centered feeling throughout the day.

There's also a subtle psychological benefit that comes with using natural elements like pink salt in your routine: the act of slowing down. Whether you're preparing a home-cooked meal, sipping warm lemon water in the morning, or soaking in a mineral bath, these rituals ask you to pause. To be present. And in today's world, that pause is often the missing ingredient in both physical and mental healing.

Perhaps what's most remarkable is how these small shifts compound over time. You may begin with pink salt for its detox or weight-loss effects, but as your digestion improves, your sleep deepens, and your energy stabilizes, you realize you're building something more profound: a lifestyle rooted in nourishment, not deprivation.

In the end, the benefits of pink Himalayan salt extend into every corner of well-being—not just trimming inches from the waistline, but restoring a deeper connection with your body, calming the mind, and supporting the kind of lasting health that doesn't show up on the scale, but is felt in every moment of daily life.

8 LIFESTYLE HABITS TO MAXIMIZE RESULTS

Adding pink Himalayan salt to your wellness journey is a powerful step—but it's just one part of a much bigger picture. To truly unlock its benefits, especially when aiming for long-term health or weight management, it's essential to pair it with daily habits that support the body as a whole. These habits don't need to be extreme or overwhelming. In fact, the most impactful changes often come from consistent, simple actions repeated every day.

One of the most important pillars is hydration. Pink salt works best in a body that is well-hydrated. When you drink water with a pinch of pink salt—particularly in the morning or after sweating—you're replenishing electrolytes and supporting everything from digestion to mental clarity. But hydration goes beyond salt water. It also means drinking enough clean water throughout the day, eating water-rich foods like cucumbers, berries, and leafy greens, and listening to your body's signals instead of waiting to feel thirsty.

Another key habit is mindful eating. In today's rushed world, meals are often consumed while scrolling through a phone or multitasking. This disconnect can lead to overeating, poor digestion, and emotional snacking. Creating a more intentional relationship with food—taking time to prepare meals, chew slowly, and eat without distractions—not only enhances nutrient absorption but also helps the body recognize fullness. When pink salt is used to flavor fresh, home-cooked meals, it naturally encourages a slower, more mindful pace that supports weight balance and digestive health.

Movement is equally important. This doesn't mean intense gym sessions every day. Instead, think in terms of joyful, regular movement—whether it's a walk in the fresh air, a morning stretch, yoga, dancing in your kitchen, or even light strength training. Exercise helps circulate lymphatic fluid, supports detoxification, reduces inflammation, and improves mood. The minerals in pink salt can assist in muscle recovery, especially when included in a post-workout drink or bath.

Sleep, often overlooked, is where much of your body's natural detox and repair occurs. Creating a sleep-friendly environment—cool, dark, and screen-free—is just as vital as any diet or detox plan. A warm evening bath with pink salt can help prepare your nervous system for deep rest, lowering cortisol levels and encouraging the kind of sleep that truly restores you.

Equally essential is stress management. Chronic stress elevates cortisol, which not only interferes with weight loss but also increases cravings and emotional eating. Incorporating calming habits like meditation, journaling, breathwork, or simply spending time in nature helps bring your nervous system back into balance. Pink salt, especially when used in grounding rituals like warm drinks, baths, or even salt lamps, can support a more relaxed, centered daily rhythm.

Finally, consistency is what turns short-term results into long-term transformation. No single day will make or break your progress. It's the steady, committed choices—choosing whole foods, staying hydrated, getting rest, moving your body, and nourishing your emotional health—that create lasting change.

Pink salt doesn't promise magic. But when paired with these supportive habits, it becomes part of a deeply sustainable approach to wellness. It's not about being perfect—it's about building a lifestyle that works with your body, not against it.

And the real reward? It's not just what you lose, but what you gain: energy, clarity, confidence, and a renewed sense of balance in both body and mind.

9 DELICIOUS RECIPES WITH PINK SALT

1. Avocado Toast with Poached Egg and Pink Salt
Calories per serving: ~195 kcal
Ingredients:
- 1 slice whole grain bread (60 kcal)
- ¼ ripe avocado (60 kcal)
- 1 poached egg (70 kcal)
- Pink Himalayan salt (a pinch)
- Pepper to taste

Instructions:
1. Toast the bread.
2. Mash the avocado and spread it on the toast.
3. Poach the egg (3–4 minutes in simmering water with a splash of vinegar).
4. Place the poached egg on the toast, season with pink salt and pepper.

---

2. Greek Yogurt with Berries, Chia Seeds, and Pink Salt Granola
Calories per serving: ~190 kcal
Ingredients:
- 100g plain non-fat Greek yogurt (60 kcal)
- 50g mixed berries (30 kcal)
- 1 tsp chia seeds (20 kcal)
- 1 tbsp homemade low-sugar pink salt granola (80 kcal)
- Pink   Himalayan   salt   (small   pinch)

Instructions:
1. Place the yogurt in a bowl.
2. Top with berries, chia seeds, and granola.
3. Add a small pinch of pink salt to enhance flavor.

---

3. Scrambled Eggs with Spinach and Pink Salt
Calories per serving: ~170 kcal
Ingredients:
- 2 egg whites + 1 whole egg (75 kcal)
- 1 cup fresh spinach (7 kcal)
- 1 tsp olive oil (40 kcal)
- Pink Himalayan salt
- Pepper to taste

Instructions:
1. Heat olive oil in a non-stick skillet.
2. Sauté spinach until wilted.
3. Beat the eggs and pour over the spinach.
4. Scramble gently, seasoning with pink salt and pepper.

---

4. Pink Salt Banana Protein Pancakes
Calories per serving (2 small pancakes): ~195 kcal
Ingredients:
- ½ banana (45 kcal)
- 1 egg (70 kcal)
- 1 tbsp oat flour (30 kcal)
- ½ scoop protein powder (vanilla) (50 kcal)
- Pinch   of   pink   salt

Instructions:
1. Mash the banana and mix with egg, oat flour, protein powder, and pink salt.
2. Cook pancakes in a non-stick pan for 2–3 minutes per side.
3. Serve plain or with a few berries if desired.

---

5. Smoothie Bowl with Coconut Flakes and Pink Salt
- Calories per serving: ~180 kcal
- Ingredients:
- ½ banana (45 kcal)
- ½ cup frozen berries (35 kcal)
- ½ cup unsweetened almond milk (15 kcal)

- 1 tsp coconut flakes (20 kcal)
- ½ tsp chia seeds (10 kcal)
- Pinch   of   pink   salt

Instructions:
1. Blend the banana, berries, almond milk, and pink salt until smooth.
2. Pour into a bowl and top with coconut flakes and chia seeds.

---

6. Oatmeal with Almond Butter, Cinnamon, and Pink Salt
Calories per serving: ~190 kcal
Ingredients:
- ¼ cup rolled oats (75 kcal)
- ½ cup water + ¼ cup almond milk (10 kcal)
- ½ tsp cinnamon
- 1 tsp almond butter (50 kcal)
- A few blueberries (10 kcal)
- Pink   salt   (small   pinch)

Instructions:
1. Cook the oats with water and almond milk until creamy.
2. Stir in cinnamon and pink salt.
3. Top with almond butter and blueberries.

---

7. Sweet Potato Hash with Red Onions and Pink Salt
Calories per serving: ~180 kcal
Ingredients.
- 100g sweet potato, diced (85 kcal)
- ¼ red onion, chopped (15 kcal)
- 1 tsp olive oil (40 kcal)
- Fresh parsley (optional)
- Pink   Himalayan   salt

Instructions:
1. Heat olive oil in a skillet, add onions, and cook until translucent.
2. Add diced sweet potato and sauté until golden and soft.
3. Season with pink salt and garnish with parsley.

---

8. Cottage Cheese and Pineapple Bowl with Pink Salt
Calories per serving: ~160 kcal
Ingredients:
- ½ cup low-fat cottage cheese (90 kcal)

- ½ cup chopped fresh pineapple (60 kcal)
- Pink   salt   (tiny   pinch)

Instructions:
1. Combine cottage cheese and pineapple in a bowl.
2. Sprinkle lightly with pink salt and mix gently.

---

9. Zucchini and Feta Omelet with Pink Salt
Calories per serving: ~185 kcal
Ingredients:
- 1 egg + 1 egg white (70 kcal)
- ¼ cup grated zucchini (5 kcal)
- 15g feta cheese (40 kcal)
- 1 tsp olive oil (40 kcal)
- Pink Himalayan salt
- Black pepper

Instructions:
1. Whisk the eggs with grated zucchini and crumbled feta.
2. Heat olive oil in a pan, pour in the mixture.
3. Cook over medium heat until set, season with pink salt and pepper.

---

10. Almond Flour Muffins with Pink Salt and Dark Chocolate Chips
Calories per muffin (mini): ~200 kcal
Ingredients:
- 3 tbsp almond flour (90 kcal)
- 1 egg (70 kcal)
- 1 tsp honey (20 kcal)
- 5g dark chocolate chips (20 kcal)
- Pink salt (pinch)
- Vanilla extract (optional)

Instructions:
1. Mix all ingredients in a bowl.
2. Pour into a muffin tin (mini size).
3. Bake at 180°C (350°F) for 12–15 minutes.
4. Cool and sprinkle lightly with pink salt.

---

11. Quinoa Salad with Chickpeas, Cucumber, Lemon, and Pink Salt
Calories per serving: ~190 kcal
Ingredients:
- ¼ cup cooked quinoa (57 kcal)

- ¼ cup chickpeas, cooked (45 kcal)
- ½ cucumber, diced (8 kcal)
- Juice of ½ lemon (5 kcal)
- 1 tsp olive oil (40 kcal)
- Pink Himalayan salt (pinch)
- Black pepper (optional)

Instructions:
1. In a large bowl, combine quinoa, chickpeas, and cucumber.
2. Drizzle with olive oil and lemon juice.
3. Season with pink salt and pepper to taste.
4. Toss well and serve chilled.

12. Watermelon, Feta, and Mint Salad with a Touch of Pink Salt
Calories per serving: ~180 kcal
Ingredients:
- 1 cup watermelon, cubed (45 kcal)
- 30g feta cheese, crumbled (80 kcal)
- 5-6 fresh mint leaves, chopped (1 kcal)
- Pink Himalayan salt (pinch)
- Black pepper (optional)

Instructions:
1. In a bowl, combine watermelon cubes, feta, and chopped mint.
2. Sprinkle lightly with pink salt and pepper.
3. Toss gently and serve chilled.

13. Arugula, Avocado, and Grapefruit Salad with Pink Salt Vinaigrette
Calories per serving: ~200 kcal
Ingredients:
- 2 cups arugula (10 kcal)
- ½ avocado, sliced (120 kcal)
- ½ grapefruit, segmented (30 kcal)
- 1 tsp olive oil (40 kcal)
- ½ tsp apple cider vinegar (1 kcal)
- Pink Himalayan salt (pinch)

Instructions:
1. In a bowl, mix arugula, avocado slices, and grapefruit segments.
2. Whisk together olive oil, apple cider vinegar, and pink salt to make the dressing.

3. Drizzle the vinaigrette over the salad, toss, and serve immediately.

14. Roasted Beet and Goat Cheese Salad with Pink Salt
Calories per serving: ~200 kcal
Ingredients:
- 1 small roasted beet, sliced (35 kcal)
- 30g goat cheese, crumbled (80 kcal)
- 1 cup mixed greens (10 kcal)
- 1 tsp balsamic vinegar (15 kcal)
- Pink Himalayan salt (pinch)
- Black pepper (optional)

Instructions:
1. Arrange roasted beet slices on a plate with mixed greens.
2. Crumble goat cheese on top.
3. Drizzle with balsamic vinegar and a pinch of pink salt.
4. Season with black pepper and serve immediately.

15. Caprese Salad with Heirloom Tomatoes and Pink Salt Flakes
Calories per serving: ~180 kcal
Ingredients:
- 1 medium heirloom tomato, sliced (22 kcal)
- 30g fresh mozzarella (70 kcal)
- 1 tsp extra virgin olive oil (40 kcal)
- Fresh basil leaves (2 kcal)
- Pink Himalayan salt flakes (pinch)

Instructions:
1. Arrange sliced heirloom tomatoes and fresh mozzarella on a plate.
2. Drizzle with olive oil and sprinkle with pink salt flakes.
3. Garnish with basil leaves and serve.

16. Grilled Peach and Burrata Salad with Honey and Pink Salt
Calories per serving: ~190 kcal
Ingredients:
- 1 medium peach, halved and grilled (40 kcal)
- 50g burrata cheese (150 kcal)
- 1 tsp honey (20 kcal)
- Pink Himalayan salt (pinch)

Instructions:

1. Grill peach halves until slightly charred.
2. Place the grilled peach halves on a plate, and top with burrata.
3. Drizzle with honey and a pinch of pink salt.
4. Serve immediately.

---

17. Kale and Cranberry Salad with Lemon-Pink Salt Dressing
Calories per serving: ~200 kcal
Ingredients:
- 2 cups kale, chopped (33 kcal)
- 2 tbsp dried cranberries (50 kcal)
- 1 tsp olive oil (40 kcal)
- Juice of ½ lemon (5 kcal)
- Pink Himalayan salt (pinch)
- Black pepper (optional)

Instructions:
1. Massage the chopped kale with olive oil until tender.
2. Add dried cranberries and mix.
3. Whisk together lemon juice, pink salt, and pepper, and drizzle over the salad.
4. Toss well and serve.

---

18. Edamame and Sesame Salad with Pink Salt
Calories per serving: ~180 kcal
Ingredients:
- 1 cup edamame, cooked (120 kcal)
- 1 tsp sesame seeds (20 kcal)
- 1 tsp rice vinegar (5 kcal)
- 1 tsp soy sauce (5 kcal)
- Pink Himalayan salt (pinch)

Instructions:
1. Cook edamame and drain well.
2. Toss edamame with sesame seeds, rice vinegar, soy sauce, and pink salt.
3. Serve chilled or at room temperature.

---

19. Lentil and Roasted Veggie Salad with Pink Salt
Calories per serving: ~200 kcal
Ingredients:
- ½ cup cooked lentils (90 kcal)

- ½ cup roasted vegetables (zucchini, bell peppers) (50 kcal)
- 1 tsp olive oil (40 kcal)
- Pink Himalayan salt (pinch)

Instructions:
1. Mix cooked lentils with roasted vegetables in a bowl.
2. Drizzle with olive oil and season with pink salt.
3. Toss and serve immediately.

---

20. Spinach and Apple Salad with Walnut-Pink Salt Crumble
Calories per serving: ~190 kcal
Ingredients:
- 2 cups fresh spinach (14 kcal)
- ½ apple, thinly sliced (30 kcal
- 1 tbsp walnuts, chopped (50 kcal)
- ½ tsp honey (10 kcal)
- Pink Himalayan salt (pinch)

Instructions:
1. Combine spinach and apple slices in a bowl.
2. In a separate pan, toast walnuts with a pinch of pink salt and honey.
3. Sprinkle the walnut crumble on top of the salad and serve immediately.

---

21. Carrot-Ginger Soup with Pink Salt
Calories per serving: ~95 kcal
Ingredients:
- 2 medium carrots, sliced (50 kcal)
- 1 tsp grated fresh ginger (2 kcal)
- 1 cup low-sodium vegetable broth (10 kcal)
- ½ tsp olive oil (20 kcal)
- Pink Himalayan salt (a pinch)
- Pepper to taste

Instructions:
1. Heat the oil in a saucepan and add the grated ginger.
2. Add the carrots and vegetable broth.
3. Simmer for 15–20 minutes until the carrots are soft.
4. Blend until smooth and creamy.
5. Season with pink salt and pepper.

22. Creamy Tomato Basil Soup with Pink Salt

Calories per serving: ~120 kcal

Ingredients:
- 1 cup canned crushed tomatoes (35 kcal)
- ¼ cup unsweetened almond milk (8 kcal)
- 1 tsp olive oil (40 kcal)
- 1 tbsp chopped fresh basil (1 kcal)
- 1 garlic clove, minced (4 kcal)
- Pink Himalayan salt (a pinch)
- Pepper to taste

Instructions:
1. In a pan, sauté the garlic in the oil for 1 minute.
2. Add the tomatoes and cook for 10 minutes.
3. Pour in the almond milk and add the basil.
4. Blend until smooth and creamy.
5. Season with pink salt and pepper.

23. Bone Broth Enhanced with Pink Himalayan Salt

Calories per serving: ~45 kcal

Ingredients:
- 1 cup organic bone broth (40 kcal)
- Pink Himalayan salt (a pinch)
- Chopped parsley (1 kcal)
- A few drops of lemon juice

Instructions:
1. Heat the broth in a small saucepan.
2. Add the lemon juice.
3. Season with pink salt and parsley.
4. Serve hot.

24. Lentil Soup with Cumin and Pink Salt

Calories per serving: ~165 kcal

Ingredients:
- ¼ cup red lentils (90 kcal)
- 1 cup water or broth (10 kcal)
- ½ tsp ground cumin (4 kcal)
- 1 tsp olive oil (40 kcal)
- 1 tbsp chopped onion (5 kcal)

- Pink Himalayan salt (a pinch)

Instructions:
1. Sauté the onion and cumin in the oil for 2 minutes.
2. Add the lentils and water.
3. Cook over medium heat for 15–20 minutes.
4. Blend if you prefer a smooth texture.
5. Adjust with pink salt.

25. Chicken and Wild Rice Soup with Pink Salt
Calories per serving: ~180 kcal
Ingredients:
- ¼ cup cooked chicken breast, shredded (60 kcal)
- 2 tbsp cooked wild rice (35 kcal)
- 1 cup chicken broth (15 kcal)
- ¼ cup diced carrots and celery (10 kcal)
- 1 tsp olive oil (40 kcal)
- Pink Himalayan salt (a pinch)
- Fresh thyme or parsley

Instructions:
1. Sauté carrots and celery in oil for 3 minutes.
2. Add the broth, chicken, and rice.
3. Simmer for 10 minutes.
4. Season with pink salt and herbs.
5. Serve hot.

26. Cauliflower and Leek Soup with a Pink Salt Crunch
Calories per serving: ~100 kcal
Ingredients:
- 1 cup cauliflower florets (25 kcal)
- ¼ cup sliced leeks (15 kcal)
- 1 tsp olive oil (40 kcal)
- 1 cup broth (10 kcal)
- ¼ tsp toasted pumpkin seeds (10 kcal)
- Pink Himalayan salt (a pinch)

Instructions:
1. Sauté the leeks in oil for 3 minutes.
2. Add the cauliflower and broth.
3. Cook for 15 minutes and blend.

4. Garnish with toasted seeds and pink salt.
5. Serve hot.

---

27. Spicy Black Bean Soup with Pink Salt
Calories per serving: ~190 kcal
Ingredients:
- ½ cup canned black beans, rinsed (100 kcal)
- 1 tsp olive oil (40 kcal)
- 1 tbsp diced onion and garlic (5 kcal)
- ½ cup broth (5 kcal)
- 1 tsp chili powder (6 kcal)
- Pink Himalayan salt (a pinch)

Instructions:
1. Sauté onion, garlic, and spices in oil.
2. Add beans and broth.
3. Cook for 10 minutes.
4. Mash or blend partially.
5. Add pink salt and serve.

---

28. Butternut Squash Soup with Coconut Milk and Pink Salt
Calories per serving: ~180 kcal
Ingredients:
- 1 cup cubed butternut squash (60 kcal)
- ½ tsp olive oil (20 kcal)
- ¼ cup light coconut milk (50 kcal)
- ½ cup vegetable broth (10 kcal)
- Pink Himalayan salt (a pinch)
- Nutmeg (optional)

Instructions:
1. Cook the pumpkin in a pan with oil for 10 minutes.
2. Add broth and cook until tender.
3. Pour in the coconut milk and blend.
4. Season with pink salt and nutmeg.
5. Serve warm.

---

29. Miso Soup with Tofu and Pink Salt Substitute
Calories per serving: ~90 kcal
Ingredients:
- 1 tsp white miso paste (15 kcal)

- ½ cup cubed silken tofu (40 kcal)
- 1 cup water (0 kcal)
- 1 tsp seaweed (3 kcal)
- Pink salt substitute (optional)
- 1 tbsp chopped green onion (2 kcal)

Instructions:
1. Heat the water without bringing it to a boil.
2. Add the miso paste and stir well.
3. Add tofu and seaweed.
4. Let it simmer for 2–3 minutes.
5. Garnish with spring onions and pink salt if desired.

30. Green Pea and Mint Soup with Pink Salt Garnish
Calories per serving: ~130 kcal
Ingredients:
- ¾ cup frozen green peas (90 kcal)
- 1 tsp olive oil (40 kcal)
- 1 tbsp fresh mint (1 kcal)
- ½ cup broth (5 kcal)
- Pink Himalayan salt (a pinch)

Instructions:
1. Sauté the peas in oil for 2 minutes.
2. Add the broth and mint, cook for 8–10 minutes.
3. Blend everything until smooth.
4. Garnish with pink salt.
5. Serve hot or warm.

31. Grilled Lemon-Herb Chicken with Pink Salt
Calories per serving: ~190 kcal
Ingredients:
- 100 g chicken breast (165 kcal)
- 1 tsp olive oil (40 kcal)
- 1 tsp lemon juice (1 kcal)
- ½ tsp dried rosemary or thyme (1 kcal)
- Pink Himalayan salt (a pinch)
- Pepper to taste

Instructions:
1. Marinate the chicken with olive oil, lemon juice, herbs, salt, and

pepper.
2. Let it rest for 15 minutes.
3. Grill on medium heat for 5–6 minutes per side.
4. Serve hot with a lemon wedge.

32. Baked Salmon with Garlic, Dill, and Pink Salt
Calories per serving: ~195 kcal
Ingredients:

- 80 g salmon fillet (160 kcal)
- 1 tsp olive oil (40 kcal)
- 1 small garlic clove, minced (4 kcal)
- ½ tsp dried dill or fresh (1 kcal)
- Pink Himalayan salt (a pinch)
- Lemon zest (optional)

Instructions:
1. Preheat the oven to 180°C (350°F).
2. Rub salmon with olive oil, garlic, dill, and pink salt.
3. Place on parchment paper and bake for 12–15 minutes.
4. Garnish with lemon zest and serve.

33. Stir-Fried Tofu with Vegetables and Pink Salt Soy Glaze
Calories per serving: ~180 kcal
Ingredients:

- 80 g firm tofu, cubed (95 kcal)
- ½ cup mixed bell peppers and zucchini (20 kcal)
- 1 tsp sesame or olive oil (40 kcal)
- 1 tsp low-sodium soy sauce (5 kcal)
- Pink Himalayan salt (a pinch)
- Garlic and ginger, minced (5 kcal)

Instructions:
1. Heat oil in a pan and sauté garlic and ginger.
2. Add tofu cubes and stir-fry until golden.
3. Add vegetables, cook for 5–6 minutes.
4. Drizzle with soy sauce and pink salt.
5. Serve warm.

34. Quinoa-Stuffed Bell Peppers with Pink Salt
Calories per serving: ~170 kcal
Ingredients:

- ½ medium bell pepper (15 kcal)
- ¼ cup cooked quinoa (57 kcal)
- 1 tbsp black beans (20 kcal)
- 1 tsp olive oil (40 kcal)
- 1 tbsp chopped tomato (5 kcal)
- Cumin, oregano, and pink Himalayan salt (a pinch)

Instructions:
1. Preheat oven to 180°C (350°F).
2. Mix quinoa, beans, tomato, and spices.
3. Stuff the bell pepper half with mixture.
4. Drizzle with oil and bake for 20 minutes.
5. Sprinkle with pink salt before serving.

35. Cauliflower "Steaks" with Chimichurri and Pink Salt
Calories per serving: ~150 kcal
Ingredients:
- 1 thick slice cauliflower (25 kcal)
- 1 tsp olive oil (40 kcal)
- 1 tbsp chimichurri (80 kcal)
- Pink Himalayan salt (a pinch)

Instructions:
1. Brush cauliflower with olive oil and pink salt.
2. Roast or grill for 10–12 minutes per side.
3. Top with chimichurri sauce.
4. Serve hot as a light main or side.

36. Sweet Potato and Black Bean Tacos with Pink Salt Crema
Calories per serving: ~195 kcal
Ingredients:
- 1 small corn tortilla (60 kcal)
- ¼ cup roasted sweet potato cubes (50 kcal)
- 1 tbsp black beans (20 kcal)
- 1 tsp Greek yogurt (10 kcal)
- ½ tsp lime juice (1 kcal)
- ½ tsp olive oil (20 kcal)
- Pinch of cumin and pink Himalayan salt

Instructions:
1. Warm the tortilla in a dry pan.

2. Mash or mix the beans and sweet potato with cumin and salt.
3. Fill the tortilla with the mixture.
4. Mix yogurt, lime juice, and salt to make crema.
5. Drizzle crema on top and serve.

---

37. Turkey Meatballs in Tomato-Pink Salt Sauce

Calories per serving: ~180 kcal (2 small meatballs + sauce)

Ingredients:

- 80 g lean ground turkey (120 kcal)
- 1 tbsp chopped onion (5 kcal)
- 1 tsp olive oil (40 kcal)
- ¼ cup tomato passata (10 kcal)
- Italian herbs and pink Himalayan salt (a pinch)

Instructions:

1. Mix turkey with onion, herbs, and salt. Form into small balls.
2. Cook in a pan with olive oil until browned.
3. Add tomato passata and simmer 10 minutes.
4. Serve hot with sauce spooned over.

---

38. Grilled Shrimp Skewers with Lime and Pink Salt

Calories per serving: ~110 kcal (4–5 shrimp)

Ingredients:

- 80 g shrimp, peeled (80 kcal)
- ½ tsp olive oil (20 kcal)
- ½ tsp lime juice (1 kcal)
- Pink Himalayan salt (a pinch)
- Chili flakes or pepper (optional)

Instructions:

1. Marinate shrimp with oil, lime juice, and salt.
2. Skewer them and grill for 2–3 minutes per side.
3. Sprinkle with extra salt and chili if desired.
4. Serve warm.

---

39. Moroccan Chickpea Stew with Pink Salt

Calories per serving: ~170 kcal

Ingredients:

- ¼ cup canned chickpeas, rinsed (70 kcal)
- ¼ cup chopped tomatoes (10 kcal)
- 1 tbsp onion and garlic mix (5 kcal)

- ½ tsp olive oil (20 kcal)
- ¼ cup chopped zucchini or carrots (15 kcal)
- Spices: cumin, cinnamon, paprika
- Pink   Himalayan   salt   (a   pinch)

Instructions:
1. Sauté onion and garlic in olive oil.
2. Add chickpeas, tomato, veggies, and spices.
3. Simmer with ¼ cup water for 15 minutes.
4. Season with pink salt and serve.

---

40. Seared Tuna Salad Bowl with Avocado and Pink Salt
Calories per serving: ~190 kcal
 Ingredients:
- 80 g seared tuna (120 kcal)
- ¼ avocado (60 kcal)
- Mixed salad greens (10 kcal)
- Lemon juice and pink Himalayan salt
- Pepper to taste

Instructions:
1. Sear the tuna for 1–2 minutes per side in a hot pan.
2. Slice and place over salad greens.
3. Add avocado slices.
4. Drizzle with lemon juice and season with pink salt.
5. Serve immediately.

---

41. Baked Kale Chips with Pink Salt
Calories per serving: ~70 kcal
 Ingredients:
- 1 cup kale leaves, stemmed and torn (30 kcal)
- 1 tsp olive oil (40 kcal)
- Pink Himalayan salt (a pinch)

Instructions:
1. Preheat oven to 160°C (325°F).
2. Toss kale with olive oil and pink salt.
3. Spread on a baking sheet in a single layer.
4. Bake for 10–15 minutes until crisp.
5. Let cool slightly and serve.

42. Roasted Sweet Potato Wedges with Paprika and Pink Salt
Calories per serving: ~130 kcal
Ingredients:
- 100 g sweet potato, sliced into wedges (90 kcal)
- 1 tsp olive oil (40 kcal)
- ¼ tsp paprika
- Pink Himalayan salt (a pinch)

Instructions:
1. Preheat oven to 200°C (400°F).
2. Toss sweet potato wedges with oil, paprika, and pink salt.
3. Place on a baking tray and roast for 20–25 minutes, flipping once.
4. Serve warm.

---

43. Hummus with Olive Oil and Pink Salt Topping
Calories per serving: ~160 kcal (3 tbsp)
Ingredients:
- 2 tbsp chickpeas (90 kcal)
- 1 tsp tahini (30 kcal)
- 1 tsp olive oil (40 kcal)
- Lemon juice, garlic, cumin (to taste)
- Pink Himalayan salt (a pinch)

Instructions:
1. Blend chickpeas, tahini, lemon juice, garlic, and cumin.
2. Add water to adjust consistency.
3. Drizzle with olive oil and sprinkle pink salt before serving.
4. Serve with raw veggie sticks.

---

44. Guacamole with Lime and Pink Salt
Calories per serving: ~120 kcal
Ingredients:
- ¼ ripe avocado (60 kcal)
- 1 tsp lime juice (1 kcal)
- 1 tbsp diced tomato and onion mix (5 kcal)
- ½ tsp olive oil (20 kcal)
- Pink Himalayan salt (a pinch)

Instructions:
1. Mash avocado with lime juice.
2. Stir in tomato, onion, and olive oil.

3. Season with pink salt.
4. Serve with sliced cucumber or carrots.

---

45. Cucumber and Dill Yogurt Dip with Pink Salt
Calories per serving: ~90 kcal
Ingredients:
- ½ cup low-fat Greek yogurt (60 kcal)
- ¼ cucumber, finely chopped (5 kcal)
- 1 tsp chopped fresh dill (1 kcal)
- ½ tsp lemon juice (1 kcal)
- Pink Himalayan salt (a pinch)

Instructions:
1. Combine yogurt, cucumber, dill, and lemon juice in a bowl.
2. Stir well and season with pink salt.
3. Chill for 15 minutes before serving.
4. Serve with raw veggie sticks or whole grain crackers.

---

46. Steamed Edamame with Crushed Pink Salt
Calories per serving: ~120 kcal
Ingredients:
- ½ cup edamame in pods (100 kcal)
- Pink Himalayan salt (a pinch), crushed

Instructions:
1. Steam edamame in boiling water for 4–5 minutes.
2. Drain and transfer to a bowl.
3. Sprinkle with crushed pink salt.
4. Serve warm or at room temperature.

---

47. Roasted Chickpeas with Garlic and Pink Salt
Calories per serving: ~140 kcal
Ingredients:
- ¼ cup canned chickpeas, rinsed and dried (90 kcal)
- 1 tsp olive oil (40 kcal)
- ¼ tsp garlic powder (3 kcal)
- Pink   Himalayan   salt   (a   pinch)

Instructions:
1. Preheat oven to 200°C (400°F).
2. Toss chickpeas with oil, garlic powder, and salt.
3. Spread on a baking sheet and roast for 20–25 minutes, shaking

halfway.
4. Let cool for a crunchy snack.

---

48. Zucchini Fritters with Pink Salt Yogurt Sauce
Calories per serving: ~180 kcal (2 fritters)
Ingredients:
- ½ medium zucchini, grated and squeezed (10 kcal)
- 1 tbsp oat flour (30 kcal)
- 1 egg white (15 kcal)
- 1 tsp olive oil (40 kcal)
- 2 tbsp Greek yogurt (20 kcal)
- Pink Himalayan salt (a pinch)
- Garlic powder and dill to taste

Instructions:
1. Mix zucchini, oat flour, egg white, and seasonings.
2. Form into 2 fritters and pan-fry in olive oil until golden.
3. Mix yogurt with salt and herbs for dipping sauce.
4. Serve warm.

---

49. Beetroot Chips with Pink Salt
Calories per serving: ~80 kcal
Ingredients:
- 1 small beetroot, thinly sliced (40 kcal)
- 1 tsp olive oil (40 kcal)
- Pink Himalayan salt (a pinch)

Instructions:
1. Preheat oven to 160°C (325°F).
2. Toss beet slices with olive oil and salt.
3. Arrange on a baking sheet in a single layer.
4. Bake for 20–25 minutes, flipping once.
5. Let cool to crisp up.

---

50. Baked Cauliflower Bites with Pink Salt
Calories per serving: ~100 kcal
Ingredients:
- 1 cup cauliflower florets (25 kcal)
- 1 tsp olive oil (40 kcal)
- ¼ tsp smoked paprika or turmeric (optional)
- Pink   Himalayan   salt   (a   pinch)

Instructions:
1. Preheat oven to 200°C (400°F).
2. Toss cauliflower with oil, spices, and salt.
3. Bake for 20–25 minutes until golden and tender.
4. Serve   warm   as   a   snack   or   side.

---

51. Dark Chocolate Bark with Almonds and Pink Salt
Calories per serving: ~180 kcal
Ingredients:
- 20 g dark chocolate 70% (110 kcal
- 1 tsp chopped almonds (30 kcal)
- Pink Himalayan salt (a pinch)

Instructions:
1. Melt the chocolate in a double boiler or microwave.
2. Spread onto parchment paper into a thin layer.
3. Sprinkle with almonds and pink salt.
4. Let cool in the fridge until solid, then break into pieces.
5. Serve 1 small piece (~25g) per portion.

---

52. Sea Salt Caramel Energy Balls with Dates and Pink Salt
Calories per serving: ~95 kcal (1 ball)
Ingredients:
- 2 Medjool dates (100 kcal)
- 1 tsp almond butter (35 kcal)
- 1 tsp oats (10 kcal)
- Pink Himalayan salt (a pinch)

Instructions:
1. Blend dates, almond butter, and oats into a sticky paste.
2. Form into small balls (makes 2 servings).
3. Sprinkle pink salt on top.
4. Chill in fridge for 30 minutes before serving.

---

53. Baked Apples with Cinnamon, Nuts, and Pink Salt
Calories per serving: ~160 kcal
Ingredients:
- ½ medium apple, sliced (45 kcal)
- 1 tsp chopped walnuts or pecans (45 kcal)
- ½ tsp cinnamon
- ½ tsp maple syrup (10 kcal)

- Pink Himalayan salt (a pinch)

Instructions:
1. Preheat oven to 180°C (350°F).
2. Place sliced apples in a baking dish.
3. Top with nuts, cinnamon, maple syrup, and pink salt.
4. Bake for 20–25 minutes until tender.
5. Serve warm.

---

54. Peanut Butter–Pink Salt Fudge
Calories per serving: ~100 kcal (1 piece)
Ingredients:
- 1 tbsp natural peanut butter (90 kcal)
- ½ tsp coconut oil (10 kcal)
- Drop of vanilla extract
- Pink Himalayan salt (a pinch)

Instructions:
1. Mix peanut butter, coconut oil, and vanilla.
2. Pour into a mini silicone mold.
3. Sprinkle with pink salt.
4. Freeze for 1 hour until set.
5. Store chilled and enjoy 1 piece per serving.

---

55. Almond–Pink Salt Granola Bars
Calories per serving: ~190 kcal (1 bar)
Ingredients:
- 2 tbsp oats (60 kcal)
- 1 tsp almond butter (35 kcal)
- 1 tsp honey (20 kcal)
- 1 tsp chopped almonds (30 kcal)
- Pink   Himalayan   salt   (a   pinch)

Instructions:
1. Mix all ingredients in a bowl.
2. Press into a small baking dish lined with parchment.
3. Chill for 1 hour until firm, then cut into bars.
4. Store in fridge; serve 1 bar per portion.

---

56. Coconut Macaroons with a Hint of Pink Salt
Calories per serving: ~95 kcal (1 macaroon)
Ingredients:

- 2 tbsp unsweetened shredded coconut (70 kcal)
- 1 egg white (15 kcal)
- ½ tsp honey (10 kcal)
- Pink Himalayan salt (a pinch)

Instructions:
1. Preheat oven to 170°C (340°F).
2. Mix all ingredients together.
3. Form into 2 small mounds on a baking sheet.
4. Bake for 12–15 minutes until golden.
5. Let cool and serve 1 macaroon per portion.

57. Pink Salt Chocolate Avocado Mousse
Calories per serving: ~180 kcal
Ingredients:
- ¼ ripe avocado (60 kcal)
- 1 tsp cocoa powder (5 kcal)
- 1 tsp maple syrup or honey (20 kcal)
- 2 tbsp almond milk (5 kcal)
- Pink Himalayan salt (a pinch)

Instructions:
1. Blend all ingredients until smooth and creamy
2. Chill in fridge for 15–20 minutes.
3. Serve in a small bowl or cup.
4. Garnish with extra salt flakes or cocoa dusting.

58. Oatmeal Cookies with Pink Salt Flakes
Calories per serving: ~95 kcal (1 cookie)
Ingredients:
- 2 tbsp oats (60 kcal)
- 1 tsp mashed banana (10 kcal)
- ½ tsp honey or maple syrup (10 kcal)
- ½ tsp coconut oil (10 kcal)
- Pink Himalayan salt flakes (a pinch)

Instructions:
1. Preheat oven to 180°C (350°F).
2. Mix all ingredients into a dough.
3. Form into 1–2 small cookies.
4. Bake for 10–12 minutes until golden.

5. Cool and sprinkle with pink salt flakes before serving.

---

59. Banana Ice Cream with Pink Salt Swirl
Calories per serving: ~120 kcal
Ingredients:
- 1 frozen ripe banana (90 kcal)
- 1 tsp almond milk (5 kcal)
- ¼ tsp maple syrup (5 kcal)
- Pink Himalayan salt (a pinch)

Instructions:
1. Blend banana and almond milk into a creamy texture.
2. Swirl in maple syrup and pink salt.
3. Freeze for 15 minutes if needed to firm.
4. Serve in a small bowl immediately.

---

60. Salted Tahini and Honey Bliss Balls
Calories per serving: ~100 kcal (1 ball)
Ingredients:
- 1 tsp tahini (30 kcal
- 1 tsp oats (10 kcal)
- 1 tsp honey (20 kcal
- 1 tsp shredded coconut (10 kcal)
- Pink Himalayan salt (a pinch)

Instructions:
1. Mix all ingredients into a dough.
2. Roll into 1–2 small balls.
3. Sprinkle with pink salt.
4. Chill   for   30   minutes   before   serving.

10 60-DAY PINK SALT WEIGHT LOSS MEAL PLAN

DAY 1:
- **Breakfast:** Pink Salt Banana Protein Pancakes – ~195 kcal
- **Snack:** Smoothie Bowl with Coconut Flakes and Pink Salt – ~180 kcal
- **Lunch:** Spinach and Apple Salad with Walnut-Pink Salt Crumble – ~190 kcal
- **Snack:** Steamed Edamame with Crushed Pink Salt – ~120 kcal
- **Dinner:** Sweet Potato and Black Bean Tacos with Pink Salt Crema – ~195 kcal
- **Dessert:** Peanut Butter–Pink Salt Fudge – ~100 kcal

Total Daily Calories: ~1,080 kcal

DAY 2:
- **Breakfast:** Scrambled Eggs with Spinach and Pink Salt – ~170 kcal
- **Snack:** Cottage Cheese and Pineapple Bowl with Pink Salt – ~160 kcal
- **Lunch:** Roasted Beet and Goat Cheese Salad with Pink Salt – ~200 kcal
- **Snack:** Guacamole with Lime and Pink Salt – ~120 kcal
- **Dinner:** Baked Salmon with Garlic, Dill, and Pink Salt – ~195 kcal
- **Dessert:** Coconut Macaroons with a Hint of Pink Salt – ~95 kcal

Total Daily Calories: ~1,040 kcal

DAY 3:

- **Breakfast:** Greek Yogurt with Berries, Chia Seeds, and Pink Salt Granola – ~190 kcal
- **Snack:** Zucchini Fritters with Pink Salt Yogurt Sauce – ~180 kcal
- **Lunch:** Caprese Salad with Heirloom Tomatoes and Pink Salt Flakes – ~180 kcal
- **Snack:** Roasted Sweet Potato Wedges with Paprika and Pink Salt – ~130 kcal
- **Dinner:** Stir-Fried Tofu with Vegetables and Pink Salt Soy Glaze – ~180 kcal
- **Dessert:** Banana Ice Cream with Pink Salt Swirl – ~120 kcal

Total Daily Calories: ~1,080 kcal

DAY 4

- **Breakfast:** Scrambled Eggs with Spinach and Pink Salt (~170 kcal)
- **Snack:** Baked Kale Chips with Pink Salt (~70 kcal)
- **Lunch:** Kale and Cranberry Salad with Lemon-Pink Salt Dressing (~200 kcal)
- **Snack:** Hummus with Olive Oil and Pink Salt Topping (~160 kcal)
- **Dinner:** Stir-Fried Tofu with Vegetables and Pink Salt Soy Glaze (~180 kcal)
- **Dessert:** Pink Salt Chocolate Avocado Mousse (~180 kcal)

Total Daily Calories: ~960 kcal

DAY 5

- **Breakfast:** Pink Salt Banana Protein Pancakes (~195 kcal)
- **Snack:** Sea Salt Caramel Energy Balls (~95 kcal)
- **Lunch:** Moroccan Chickpea Stew with Pink Salt (~170 kcal)
- **Snack:** Cucumber and Dill Yogurt Dip with Pink Salt (~90 kcal)
- **Dinner:** Baked Salmon with Garlic, Dill, and Pink Salt (~195 kcal)
- **Dessert:** Coconut Macaroons with a Hint of Pink Salt (~95 kcal)

Total Daily Calories: ~940 kcal

DAY 6

- **Breakfast:** Oatmeal with Almond Butter, Cinnamon, and Pink Salt (~190 kcal)
- **Snack:** Roasted Chickpeas with Garlic and Pink Salt (~140 kcal)
- **Lunch:** Caprese Salad with Heirloom Tomatoes and Pink Salt Flakes (~180 kcal)
- **Snack:** Guacamole with Lime and Pink Salt (~120 kcal)
- **Dinner:** Chicken and Wild Rice Soup with Pink Salt (~180 kcal)
- **Dessert:** Peanut Butter–Pink Salt Fudge (~100 kcal)

Total Daily Calories: ~910 kcal

DAY 7
- **Breakfast:** Cottage Cheese and Pineapple Bowl with Pink Salt (~160 kcal)
- **Snack:** Baked Cauliflower Bites with Pink Salt (~100 kcal)
- **Lunch:** Lentil and Roasted Veggie Salad with Pink Salt (~200 kcal)
- **Snack:** Steamed Edamame with Crushed Pink Salt (~120 kcal)
- **Dinner:** Cauliflower "Steaks" with Chimichurri and Pink Salt (~150 kcal)
- **Dessert:** Banana Ice Cream with Pink Salt Swirl (~120 kcal)

Total Daily Calories: ~850 kcal

DAY 8
- **Breakfast:** Smoothie Bowl with Coconut Flakes and Pink Salt (~180 kcal)
- **Snack:** Dark Chocolate Bark with Almonds and Pink Salt (~180 kcal)
- **Lunch:** Roasted Beet and Goat Cheese Salad with Pink Salt (~200 kcal)
- **Snack:** Zucchini Fritters with Pink Salt Yogurt Sauce (~180 kcal)
- **Dinner:** Turkey Meatballs in Tomato-Pink Salt Sauce (~180 kcal)
- **Dessert:** Salted Tahini and Honey Bliss Balls (~100 kcal)

Total Daily Calories: ~1,020 kcal

DAY 9
- **Breakfast:** Greek Yogurt with Berries, Chia Seeds, and Pink Salt Granola (~190 kcal)
- **Snack:** Sea Salt Caramel Energy Balls (~95 kcal)
- **Lunch:** Arugula, Avocado, and Grapefruit Salad with Pink Salt Vinaigrette (~200 kcal)
- **Snack:** Hummus with Olive Oil and Pink Salt Topping (~160 kcal)
- **Dinner:** Grilled Lemon-Herb Chicken with Pink Salt (~190 kcal)
- **Dessert:** Baked Apples with Cinnamon, Nuts, and Pink Salt (~160 kcal)

Total Daily Calories: ~1,005 kcal

DAY 10
- **Breakfast:** Almond Flour Muffins with Pink Salt and Dark Chocolate Chips (~200 kcal)
- **Snack:** Roasted Sweet Potato Wedges with Paprika and Pink Salt

(~130 kcal)
- **Lunch:** Quinoa Salad with Chickpeas, Cucumber, Lemon, and Pink Salt (~190 kcal)
- **Snack:** Steamed Edamame with Crushed Pink Salt (~120 kcal)
- **Dinner:** Grilled Shrimp Skewers with Lime and Pink Salt (~110 kcal)
- **Dessert:** Oatmeal Cookies with Pink Salt Flakes (~95 kcal)

Total Daily Calories: ~845 kcal

DAY 11
- **Breakfast:** Scrambled Eggs with Spinach and Pink Salt (~170 kcal)
- **Snack:** Roasted Chickpeas with Garlic and Pink Salt (~140 kcal)
- **Lunch:** Lentil Soup with Cumin and Pink Salt (~165 kcal)
- **Snack:** Guacamole with Lime and Pink Salt (~120 kcal)
- **Dinner:** Quinoa-Stuffed Bell Peppers with Pink Salt (~170 kcal)
- **Dessert:** Peanut Butter–Pink Salt Fudge (~100 kcal)

Total Daily Calories: ~865 kcal

DAY 12
- **Breakfast:** Pink Salt Banana Protein Pancakes (~195 kcal)
- **Snack:** Coconut Macaroons with a Hint of Pink Salt (~95 kcal)
- **Lunch:** Spinach and Apple Salad with Walnut-Pink Salt Crumble (~190 kcal)
- **Snack:** Cucumber and Dill Yogurt Dip with Pink Salt (~90 kcal)
- **Dinner:** Butternut Squash Soup with Coconut Milk and Pink Salt (~180 kcal)
- **Dessert:** Banana Ice Cream with Pink Salt Swirl (~120 kcal)

Total Daily Calories: ~870 kcal

DAY 13
- **Breakfast:** Avocado Toast with Poached Egg and Pink Salt (~195 kcal)
- **Snack:** Baked Kale Chips with Pink Salt (~70 kcal)
- **Lunch:** Edamame and Sesame Salad with Pink Salt (~180 kcal)
- **Snack:** Guacamole with Lime and Pink Salt (~120 kcal)
- **Dinner:** Miso Soup with Tofu and Pink Salt Substitute (~90 kcal)
- **Dessert:** Salted Tahini and Honey Bliss Balls (~100 kcal)

Total Daily Calories: ~755 kcal

DAY 14
- **Breakfast:** Oatmeal with Almond Butter, Cinnamon, and Pink Salt

(~190 kcal)
- **Snack:** Sea Salt Caramel Energy Balls (~95 kcal)
- **Lunch:** Caprese Salad with Heirloom Tomatoes and Pink Salt Flakes (~180 kcal)
- **Snack:** Hummus with Olive Oil and Pink Salt Topping (~160 kcal)
- **Dinner:** Cauliflower and Leek Soup with a Pink Salt Crunch (~100 kcal)
- **Dessert:** Pink Salt Chocolate Avocado Mousse (~180 kcal)

Total Daily Calories: ~905 kcal

Day 15:
- **Breakfast:** Avocado Toast with Poached Egg and Pink Salt – ~195 kcal
- **Snack:** Greek Yogurt with Berries, Chia Seeds, and Pink Salt Granola – ~190 kcal
- **Lunch:** Quinoa Salad with Chickpeas, Cucumber, Lemon, and Pink Salt – ~190 kcal
- **Snack:** Roasted Chickpeas with Garlic and Pink Salt – ~140 kcal
- **Dinner:** Grilled Lemon-Herb Chicken with Pink Salt – ~190 kcal
- **Dessert:** Dark Chocolate Bark with Almonds and Pink Salt – ~180 kcal

Total Daily Calories: ~1,095 kcal

Day 16:
- **Breakfast:** Pink Salt Banana Protein Pancakes – ~195 kcal
- **Snack:** Smoothie Bowl with Coconut Flakes and Pink Salt – ~180 kcal
- **Lunch:** Spinach and Apple Salad with Walnut-Pink Salt Crumble – ~190 kcal
- **Snack:** Steamed Edamame with Crushed Pink Salt – ~120 kcal
- **Dinner:** Sweet Potato and Black Bean Tacos with Pink Salt Crema – ~195 kcal
- **Dessert:** Peanut Butter–Pink Salt Fudge – ~100 kcal

Total Daily Calories: ~1,080 kcal

Day 17:
- **Breakfast:** Scrambled Eggs with Spinach and Pink Salt – ~170 kcal
- **Snack:** Cottage Cheese and Pineapple Bowl with Pink Salt – ~160 kcal
- **Lunch:** Roasted Beet and Goat Cheese Salad with Pink Salt – ~200 kcal
- **Snack:** Guacamole with Lime and Pink Salt – ~120 kcal

- **Dinner:** Baked Salmon with Garlic, Dill, and Pink Salt – ~195 kcal
- **Dessert:** Coconut Macaroons with a Hint of Pink Salt – ~95 kcal

Total Daily Calories: ~1,040 kcal

Day 18:

- **Breakfast:** Greek Yogurt with Berries, Chia Seeds, and Pink Salt Granola – ~190 kcal
- **Snack:** Zucchini Fritters with Pink Salt Yogurt Sauce – ~180 kcal
- **Lunch:** Caprese Salad with Heirloom Tomatoes and Pink Salt Flakes – ~180 kcal
- **Snack:** Roasted Sweet Potato Wedges with Paprika and Pink Salt – ~130 kcal
- **Dinner:** Stir-Fried Tofu with Vegetables and Pink Salt Soy Glaze – ~180 kcal
- **Dessert:** Banana Ice Cream with Pink Salt Swirl – ~120 kcal

Total Daily Calories: ~1,080 kcal

Day 19:

- **Breakfast:** Oatmeal with Almond Butter, Cinnamon, and Pink Salt – ~190 kcal
- **Snack:** Hummus with Olive Oil and Pink Salt Topping – ~160 kcal
- **Lunch:** Kale and Cranberry Salad with Lemon-Pink Salt Dressing – ~200 kcal
- **Snack:** Roasted Chickpeas with Garlic and Pink Salt – ~140 kcal
- **Dinner:** Grilled Shrimp Skewers with Lime and Pink Salt – ~110 kcal
- **Dessert:** Sea Salt Caramel Energy Balls with Dates and Pink Salt – ~95 kcal

Total Daily Calories: ~895 kcal

Day 20:

- **Breakfast:** Smoothie Bowl with Coconut Flakes and Pink Salt – ~180 kcal
- **Snack:** Almond Flour Muffins with Pink Salt and Dark Chocolate Chips – ~200 kcal
- **Lunch:** Roasted Sweet Potato and Feta Salad with Pink Salt – ~190 kcal
- **Snack:** Zucchini Fritters with Pink Salt Yogurt Sauce – ~180 kcal
- **Dinner:** Grilled Lemon-Herb Chicken with Pink Salt – ~190 kcal
- **Dessert:** Pink Salt Chocolate Avocado Mousse – ~180 kcal

Total Daily Calories: ~1,120 kcal

Day 21:
- **Breakfast:** Avocado Toast with Poached Egg and Pink Salt – ~195 kcal
- **Snack:** Greek Yogurt with Berries, Chia Seeds, and Pink Salt Granola – ~190 kcal
- **Lunch:** Lentil Soup with Cumin and Pink Salt – ~165 kcal
- **Snack:** Roasted Chickpeas with Garlic and Pink Salt – ~140 kcal
- **Dinner:** Baked Salmon with Garlic, Dill, and Pink Salt – ~195 kcal
- **Dessert:** Almond–Pink Salt Granola Bars – ~190 kcal

Total Daily Calories: ~1,085 kcal

Day 22:
- **Breakfast:** Pink Salt Banana Protein Pancakes – ~195 kcal
- **Snack:** Smoothie Bowl with Coconut Flakes and Pink Salt – ~180 kcal
- **Lunch:** Quinoa Salad with Chickpeas, Cucumber, Lemon, and Pink Salt – ~190 kcal
- **Snack:** Steamed Edamame with Crushed Pink Salt – ~120 kcal
- **Dinner:** Grilled Lemon-Herb Chicken with Pink Salt – ~190 kcal
- **Dessert:** Dark Chocolate Bark with Almonds and Pink Salt – ~180 kcal

Total Daily Calories: ~1,085 kcal

Day 23:
- **Breakfast:** Scrambled Eggs with Spinach and Pink Salt – ~170 kcal
- **Snack:** Cottage Cheese and Pineapple Bowl with Pink Salt – ~160 kcal
- **Lunch:** Roasted Beet and Goat Cheese Salad with Pink Salt – ~200 kcal
- **Snack:** Hummus with Olive Oil and Pink Salt Topping – ~160 kcal
- **Dinner:** Sweet Potato and Black Bean Tacos with Pink Salt Crema – ~195 kcal
- **Dessert:** Sea Salt Caramel Energy Balls with Dates and Pink Salt – ~95 kcal

Total Daily Calories: ~1,080 kcal

Day 24:
- **Breakfast:** Greek Yogurt with Berries, Chia Seeds, and Pink Salt Granola – ~190 kcal
- **Snack:** Zucchini Fritters with Pink Salt Yogurt Sauce – ~180 kcal
- **Lunch:** Spinach and Apple Salad with Walnut-Pink Salt Crumble – ~190 kcal

- **Snack:** Roasted Sweet Potato Wedges with Paprika and Pink Salt – ~130 kcal
- **Dinner:** Baked Salmon with Garlic, Dill, and Pink Salt – ~195 kcal
- **Dessert:** Pink Salt Chocolate Avocado Mousse – ~180 kcal

Total Daily Calories: ~1,085 kcal

Day 25:

- **Breakfast:** Oatmeal with Almond Butter, Cinnamon, and Pink Salt – ~190 kcal
- **Snack:** Roasted Chickpeas with Garlic and Pink Salt – ~140 kcal
- **Lunch:** Quinoa Salad with Chickpeas, Cucumber, Lemon, and Pink Salt – ~190 kcal
- **Snack:** Steamed Edamame with Crushed Pink Salt – ~120 kcal
- **Dinner:** Grilled Shrimp Skewers with Lime and Pink Salt – ~110 kcal
- **Dessert:** Peanut Butter–Pink Salt Fudge – ~100 kcal

Total Daily Calories: ~850 kcal

Day 26:

- **Breakfast:** Smoothie Bowl with Coconut Flakes and Pink Salt – ~180 kcal
- **Snack:** Almond Flour Muffins with Pink Salt and Dark Chocolate Chips – ~200 kcal
- **Lunch:** Caprese Salad with Heirloom Tomatoes and Pink Salt Flakes – ~180 kcal
- **Snack:** Zucchini Fritters with Pink Salt Yogurt Sauce – ~180 kcal
- **Dinner:** Stir-Fried Tofu with Vegetables and Pink Salt Soy Glaze – ~180 kcal
- **Dessert:** Coconut Macaroons with a Hint of Pink Salt – ~95 kcal

Total Daily Calories: ~1,015 kcal

Day 27:

- **Breakfast:** Avocado Toast with Poached Egg and Pink Salt – ~195 kcal
- **Snack:** Greek Yogurt with Berries, Chia Seeds, and Pink Salt Granola – ~190 kcal
- **Lunch:** Kale and Cranberry Salad with Lemon-Pink Salt Dressing – ~200 kcal
- **Snack:** Roasted Sweet Potato Wedges with Paprika and Pink Salt – ~130 kcal
- **Dinner:** Grilled Lemon-Herb Chicken with Pink Salt – ~190 kcal
- **Dessert:** Sea Salt Caramel Energy Balls with Dates and Pink Salt –

~95 kcal
Total Daily Calories: ~1,030 kcal

Day 28:

- **Breakfast:** Pink Salt Banana Protein Pancakes – ~195 kcal
- **Snack:** Smoothie Bowl with Coconut Flakes and Pink Salt – ~180 kcal
- **Lunch:** Roasted Beet and Goat Cheese Salad with Pink Salt – ~200 kcal
- **Snack:** Guacamole with Lime and Pink Salt – ~120 kcal
- **Dinner:** Baked Salmon with Garlic, Dill, and Pink Salt – ~195 kcal
- **Dessert:** Almond–Pink Salt Granola Bars – ~190 kcal

Total Daily Calories: ~1,080 kcal

Day 29:

- **Breakfast:** Scrambled Eggs with Spinach and Pink Salt – ~170 kcal
- **Snack:** Cottage Cheese and Pineapple Bowl with Pink Salt – ~160 kcal
- **Lunch:** Quinoa-Stuffed Bell Peppers with Pink Salt – ~170 kcal
- **Snack:** Hummus with Olive Oil and Pink Salt Topping – ~160 kcal
- **Dinner:** Grilled Shrimp Skewers with Lime and Pink Salt – ~110 kcal
- **Dessert:** Dark Chocolate Bark with Almonds and Pink Salt – ~180 kcal

Total Daily Calories: ~950 kcal

Day 30:

- **Breakfast:** Greek Yogurt with Berries, Chia Seeds, and Pink Salt Granola – ~190 kcal
- **Snack:** Roasted Chickpeas with Garlic and Pink Salt – ~140 kcal
- **Lunch:** Caprese Salad with Heirloom Tomatoes and Pink Salt Flakes – ~180 kcal
- **Snack:** Steamed Edamame with Crushed Pink Salt – ~120 kcal
- **Dinner:** Sweet Potato and Black Bean Tacos with Pink Salt Crema – ~195 kcal
- **Dessert:** Coconut Macaroons with a Hint of Pink Salt – ~95 kcal

Total Daily Calories: ~1,020 kcal

Day 31:

- **Breakfast:** Avocado Toast with Poached Egg and Pink Salt – ~195 kcal
- **Snack:** Greek Yogurt with Berries, Chia Seeds, and Pink Salt

Granola – ~190 kcal
- **Lunch:** Roasted Beet and Goat Cheese Salad with Pink Salt – ~200 kcal
- **Snack:** Zucchini Fritters with Pink Salt Yogurt Sauce – ~180 kcal
- **Dinner:** Stir-Fried Tofu with Vegetables and Pink Salt Soy Glaze – ~180 kcal
- **Dessert:** Sea Salt Caramel Energy Balls with Dates and Pink Salt – ~95 kcal

Total Daily Calories: ~1,040 kcal

Day 32:
- **Breakfast:** Oatmeal with Almond Butter, Cinnamon, and Pink Salt – ~190 kcal
- **Snack:** Roasted Sweet Potato Wedges with Paprika and Pink Salt – ~130 kcal
- **Lunch:** Quinoa Salad with Chickpeas, Cucumber, Lemon, and Pink Salt – ~190 kcal
- **Snack:** Steamed Edamame with Crushed Pink Salt – ~120 kcal
- **Dinner:** Baked Salmon with Garlic, Dill, and Pink Salt – ~195 kcal
- **Dessert:** Pink Salt Chocolate Avocado Mousse – ~180 kcal

Total Daily Calories: ~1,015 kcal

Day 33:
- **Breakfast:** Smoothie Bowl with Coconut Flakes and Pink Salt – ~180 kcal
- **Snack:** Almond Flour Muffins with Pink Salt and Dark Chocolate Chips – ~200 kcal
- **Lunch:** Kale and Cranberry Salad with Lemon-Pink Salt Dressing – ~200 kcal
- **Snack:** Roasted Chickpeas with Garlic and Pink Salt – ~140 kcal
- **Dinner:** Grilled Lemon-Herb Chicken with Pink Salt – ~190 kcal
- **Dessert:** Banana Ice Cream with Pink Salt Swirl – ~120 kcal

Total Daily Calories: ~1,030 kcal

Day 34:
- **Breakfast:** Pink Salt Banana Protein Pancakes – ~195 kcal
- **Snack:** Cottage Cheese and Pineapple Bowl with Pink Salt – ~160 kcal
- **Lunch:** Lentil Soup with Cumin and Pink Salt – ~165 kcal
- **Snack:** Steamed Edamame with Crushed Pink Salt – ~120 kcal
- **Dinner:** Grilled Shrimp Skewers with Lime and Pink Salt – ~110 kcal

- **Dessert:** Almond–Pink Salt Granola Bars – ~190 kcal

Total Daily Calories: ~980 kcal

Day 35:
- **Breakfast:** Scrambled Eggs with Spinach and Pink Salt – ~170 kcal
- **Snack:** Zucchini Fritters with Pink Salt Yogurt Sauce – ~180 kcal
- **Lunch:** Roasted Beet and Goat Cheese Salad with Pink Salt – ~200 kcal
- **Snack:** Roasted Sweet Potato Wedges with Paprika and Pink Salt – ~130 kcal
- **Dinner:** Sweet Potato and Black Bean Tacos with Pink Salt Crema – ~195 kcal
- **Dessert:** Coconut Macaroons with a Hint of Pink Salt – ~95 kcal

Total Daily Calories: ~1,070 kcal

Day 36:
- **Breakfast:** Greek Yogurt with Berries, Chia Seeds, and Pink Salt Granola – ~190 kcal
- **Snack:** Steamed Edamame with Crushed Pink Salt – ~120 kcal
- **Lunch:** Spinach and Apple Salad with Walnut-Pink Salt Crumble – ~190 kcal
- **Snack:** Hummus with Olive Oil and Pink Salt Topping – ~160 kcal
- **Dinner:** Grilled Lemon-Herb Chicken with Pink Salt – ~190 kcal
- **Dessert:** Sea Salt Caramel Energy Balls with Dates and Pink Salt – ~95 kcal

Total Daily Calories: ~1,025 kcal

Day 37:
- **Breakfast:** Avocado Toast with Poached Egg and Pink Salt – ~195 kcal
- **Snack:** Greek Yogurt with Berries, Chia Seeds, and Pink Salt Granola – ~190 kcal
- **Lunch:** Quinoa Salad with Chickpeas, Cucumber, Lemon, and Pink Salt – ~190 kcal
- **Snack:** Hummus with Olive Oil and Pink Salt Topping – ~160 kcal
- **Dinner:** Grilled Lemon-Herb Chicken with Pink Salt – ~190 kcal
- **Dessert:** Sea Salt Caramel Energy Balls with Dates and Pink Salt – ~95 kcal

Total Daily Calories: ~1,030 kcal

Day 38:
- **Breakfast:** Pink Salt Banana Protein Pancakes – ~195 kcal

- **Snack:** Cottage Cheese and Pineapple Bowl with Pink Salt – ~160 kcal
- **Lunch:** Roasted Beet and Goat Cheese Salad with Pink Salt – ~200 kcal
- **Snack:** Steamed Edamame with Crushed Pink Salt – ~120 kcal
- **Dinner:** Stir-Fried Tofu with Vegetables and Pink Salt Soy Glaze – ~180 kcal
- **Dessert:** Almond–Pink Salt Granola Bars – ~190 kcal

Total Daily Calories: ~1,045 kcal

Day 39:
- **Breakfast:** Smoothie Bowl with Coconut Flakes and Pink Salt – ~180 kcal
- **Snack:** Zucchini Fritters with Pink Salt Yogurt Sauce – ~180 kcal
- **Lunch:** Caprese Salad with Heirloom Tomatoes and Pink Salt Flakes – ~180 kcal
- **Snack:** Roasted Sweet Potato Wedges with Paprika and Pink Salt – ~130 kcal
- **Dinner:** Grilled Shrimp Skewers with Lime and Pink Salt – ~110 kcal
- **Dessert:** Peanut Butter–Pink Salt Fudge – ~100 kcal

Total Daily Calories: ~880 kcal

Day 40:
- **Breakfast:** Oatmeal with Almond Butter, Cinnamon, and Pink Salt – ~190 kcal
- **Snack:** Roasted Chickpeas with Garlic and Pink Salt – ~140 kcal
- **Lunch:** Spinach and Apple Salad with Walnut-Pink Salt Crumble – ~190 kcal
- **Snack:** Guacamole with Lime and Pink Salt – ~120 kcal
- **Dinner:** Baked Salmon with Garlic, Dill, and Pink Salt – ~195 kcal
- **Dessert:** Coconut Macaroons with a Hint of Pink Salt – ~95 kcal

Total Daily Calories: ~1,030 kcal

Day 41:
- **Breakfast:** Scrambled Eggs with Spinach and Pink Salt – ~170 kcal
- **Snack:** Greek Yogurt with Berries, Chia Seeds, and Pink Salt Granola – ~190 kcal
- **Lunch:** Quinoa-Stuffed Bell Peppers with Pink Salt – ~170 kcal
- **Snack:** Steamed Edamame with Crushed Pink Salt – ~120 kcal
- **Dinner:** Grilled Lemon-Herb Chicken with Pink Salt – ~190 kcal
- **Dessert:** Pink Salt Chocolate Avocado Mousse – ~180 kcal

Total Daily Calories: ~1,030 kcal

Day 42:
- **Breakfast:** Avocado Toast with Poached Egg and Pink Salt – ~195 kcal
- **Snack:** Almond Flour Muffins with Pink Salt and Dark Chocolate Chips – ~200 kcal
- **Lunch:** Roasted Beet and Goat Cheese Salad with Pink Salt – ~200 kcal
- **Snack:** Zucchini Fritters with Pink Salt Yogurt Sauce – ~180 kcal
- **Dinner:** Sweet Potato and Black Bean Tacos with Pink Salt Crema – ~195 kcal
- **Dessert:** Baked Apples with Cinnamon, Nuts, and Pink Salt – ~160 kcal

Total Daily Calories: ~1,130 kcal

Day 43:
- **Breakfast:** Smoothie Bowl with Coconut Flakes and Pink Salt – ~180 kcal
- **Snack:** Cucumber and Dill Yogurt Dip with Pink Salt – ~90 kcal
- **Lunch:** Arugula, Avocado, and Grapefruit Salad with Pink Salt Vinaigrette – ~200 kcal
- **Snack:** Roasted Chickpeas with Garlic and Pink Salt – ~140 kcal
- **Dinner:** Baked Salmon with Garlic, Dill, and Pink Salt – ~195 kcal
- **Dessert:** Banana Ice Cream with Pink Salt Swirl – ~120 kcal

Total Daily Calories: ~925 kcal

Day 44:
- **Breakfast:** Oatmeal with Almond Butter, Cinnamon, and Pink Salt – ~190 kcal
- **Snack:** Almond–Pink Salt Granola Bars – ~190 kcal
- **Lunch:** Lentil and Roasted Veggie Salad with Pink Salt – ~200 kcal
- **Snack:** Steamed Edamame with Crushed Pink Salt – ~120 kcal
- **Dinner:** Quinoa-Stuffed Bell Peppers with Pink Salt – ~170 kcal
- **Dessert:** Coconut Macaroons with a Hint of Pink Salt – ~95 kcal

Total Daily Calories: ~1,075 kcal

Day 45:
- **Breakfast:** Pink Salt Banana Protein Pancakes – ~195 kcal
- **Snack:** Greek Yogurt with Berries, Chia Seeds, and Pink Salt Granola – ~190 kcal
- **Lunch:** Watermelon, Feta, and Mint Salad with a Touch of Pink Salt

- – ~180 kcal
- **Snack:** Roasted Sweet Potato Wedges with Paprika and Pink Salt – ~130 kcal
- **Dinner:** Grilled Shrimp Skewers with Lime and Pink Salt – ~110 kcal
- **Dessert:** Sea Salt Caramel Energy Balls with Dates and Pink Salt – ~95 kcal

Total Daily Calories: ~900 kcal

Day 46:
- **Breakfast:** Scrambled Eggs with Spinach and Pink Salt – ~170 kcal
- **Snack:** Zucchini Fritters with Pink Salt Yogurt Sauce – ~180 kcal
- **Lunch:** Caprese Salad with Heirloom Tomatoes and Pink Salt Flakes – ~180 kcal
- **Snack:** Hummus with Olive Oil and Pink Salt Topping – ~160 kcal
- **Dinner:** Baked Kale Chips with Pink Salt – ~70 kcal
- **Dessert:** Dark chocolate bark with almonds and pink salt – ~180 kcal

Total Daily Calories: ~1,040 kcal

Day 47:
- **Breakfast:** Avocado Toast with Poached Egg and Pink Salt – ~195 kcal
- **Snack:** Cottage Cheese and Pineapple Bowl with Pink Salt – ~160 kcal
- **Lunch:** Spinach and Apple Salad with Walnut-Pink Salt Crumble – ~190 kcal
- **Snack:** Guacamole with Lime and Pink Salt – ~120 kcal
- **Dinner:** Stir-Fried Tofu with Vegetables and Pink Salt Soy Glaze – ~180 kcal
- **Dessert:** Oatmeal Cookies with Pink Salt Flakes – ~95 kcal

Total Daily Calories: ~1,040 kcal

Day 48:
- **Breakfast:** Smoothie Bowl with Coconut Flakes and Pink Salt – ~180 kcal
- **Snack:** Roasted Chickpeas with Garlic and Pink Salt – ~140 kcal
- **Lunch:** Quinoa Salad with Chickpeas, Cucumber, Lemon, and Pink Salt – ~190 kcal
- **Snack:** Steamed Edamame with Crushed Pink Salt – ~120 kcal
- **Dinner:** Grilled Lemon-Herb Chicken with Pink Salt – ~190 kcal
- **Dessert:** Pink Salt Chocolate Avocado Mousse – ~180 kcal

Total Daily Calories: ~1,000 kcal

Day 49:
- **Breakfast:** Oatmeal with Almond Butter, Cinnamon, and Pink Salt – ~190 kcal
- **Snack:** Almond–Pink Salt Granola Bars – ~190 kcal
- **Lunch:** Kale and Cranberry Salad with Lemon-Pink Salt Dressing – ~200 kcal
- **Snack:** Roasted Sweet Potato Wedges with Paprika and Pink Salt – ~130 kcal
- **Dinner:** Baked Salmon with Garlic, Dill, and Pink Salt – ~195 kcal
- **Dessert:** Peanut Butter–Pink Salt Fudge – ~100 kcal

Total Daily Calories: ~1,035 kcal

Day 50:
- **Breakfast:** Scrambled Eggs with Spinach and Pink Salt – ~170 kcal
- **Snack:** Zucchini Fritters with Pink Salt Yogurt Sauce – ~180 kcal
- **Lunch:** Roasted Beet and Goat Cheese Salad with Pink Salt – ~200 kcal
- **Snack:** Cucumber and Dill Yogurt Dip with Pink Salt – ~90 kcal
- **Dinner:** Seared Tuna Salad Bowl with Avocado and Pink Salt – ~190 kcal
- **Dessert:** Baked Apples with Cinnamon, Nuts, and Pink Salt – ~160 kcal

Total Daily Calories: ~1,030 kcal

Day 51:
- **Breakfast:** Pink Salt Banana Protein Pancakes – ~195 kcal
- **Snack:** Greek Yogurt with Berries, Chia Seeds, and Pink Salt Granola – ~190 kcal
- **Lunch:** Arugula, Avocado, and Grapefruit Salad with Pink Salt Vinaigrette – ~200 kcal
- **Snack:** Roasted Chickpeas with Garlic and Pink Salt – ~140 kcal
- **Dinner:** Grilled Shrimp Skewers with Lime and Pink Salt – ~110 kcal
- **Dessert:** Pink Salt Chocolate Avocado Mousse – ~180 kcal

Total Daily Calories: ~1,015 kcal

Day 52:
- **Breakfast:** Smoothie Bowl with Coconut Flakes and Pink Salt – ~180 kcal
- **Snack:** Steamed Edamame with Crushed Pink Salt – ~120 kcal

- **Lunch:** Quinoa-Stuffed Bell Peppers with Pink Salt – ~170 kcal
- **Snack:** Zucchini Fritters with Pink Salt Yogurt Sauce – ~180 kcal
- **Dinner:** Baked Kale Chips with Pink Salt – ~70 kcal
- **Dessert:** Dark chocolate bark with almonds and pink salt – ~180 kcal

Total Daily Calories: ~1,020 kcal

Day 53:
- **Breakfast:** Avocado Toast with Poached Egg and Pink Salt – ~195 kcal
- **Snack:** Cottage Cheese and Pineapple Bowl with Pink Salt – ~160 kcal
- **Lunch:** Lentil and Roasted Veggie Salad with Pink Salt – ~200 kcal
- **Snack:** Guacamole with Lime and Pink Salt – ~120 kcal
- **Dinner:** Stir-Fried Tofu with Vegetables and Pink Salt Soy Glaze – ~180 kcal
- **Dessert:** Coconut Macaroons with a Hint of Pink Salt – ~95 kcal

Total Daily Calories: ~1,030 kcal

Day 54:
- **Breakfast:** Scrambled Eggs with Spinach and Pink Salt – ~170 kcal
- **Snack:** Almond–Pink Salt Granola Bars – ~190 kcal
- **Lunch:** Watermelon, Feta, and Mint Salad with a Touch of Pink Salt – ~180 kcal
- **Snack:** Roasted Sweet Potato Wedges with Paprika and Pink Salt – ~130 kcal
- **Dinner:** Grilled Lemon-Herb Chicken with Pink Salt – ~190 kcal
- **Dessert:** Sea Salt Caramel Energy Balls with Dates and Pink Salt – ~95 kcal

Total Daily Calories: ~1,005 kcal

Day 55:
- **Breakfast:** Pink Salt Banana Protein Pancakes – ~195 kcal
- **Snack:** Hummus with Olive Oil and Pink Salt Topping – ~160 kcal
- **Lunch:** Roasted Beet and Goat Cheese Salad with Pink Salt – ~200 kcal
- **Snack:** Steamed Edamame with Crushed Pink Salt – ~120 kcal
- **Dinner:** Turkey Meatballs in Tomato-Pink Salt Sauce – ~180 kcal
- **Dessert:** Peanut Butter–Pink Salt Fudge – ~100 kcal

Total Daily Calories: ~1,005 kcal

Day 56:

- **Breakfast:** Oatmeal with Almond Butter, Cinnamon, and Pink Salt – ~190 kcal
- **Snack:** Beetroot Chips with Pink Salt – ~80 kcal
- **Lunch:** Quinoa Salad with Chickpeas, Cucumber, Lemon, and Pink Salt – ~190 kcal
- **Snack:** Roasted Chickpeas with Garlic and Pink Salt – ~140 kcal
- **Dinner:** Cauliflower and Leek Soup with a Pink Salt Crunch – ~100 kcal
- **Dessert:** Salted Tahini and Honey Bliss Balls – ~100 kcal

Total Daily Calories: ~800 kcal

Day 57:

- **Breakfast:** Smoothie Bowl with Coconut Flakes and Pink Salt – ~180 kcal
- **Snack:** Almond–Pink Salt Granola Bars – ~190 kcal
- **Lunch:** Caprese Salad with Heirloom Tomatoes and Pink Salt Flakes – ~180 kcal
- **Snack:** Zucchini Fritters with Pink Salt Yogurt Sauce – ~180 kcal
- **Dinner:** Grilled Shrimp Skewers with Lime and Pink Salt – ~110 kcal
- **Dessert:** Coconut Macaroons with a Hint of Pink Salt – ~95 kcal

Total Daily Calories: ~935 kcal

Day 58:

- **Breakfast:** Greek Yogurt with Berries, Chia Seeds, and Pink Salt Granola – ~190 kcal
- **Snack:** Roasted Sweet Potato Wedges with Paprika and Pink Salt – ~130 kcal
- **Lunch:** Spinach and Apple Salad with Walnut-Pink Salt Crumble – ~190 kcal
- **Snack:** Cucumber and Dill Yogurt Dip with Pink Salt – ~90 kcal
- **Dinner:** Grilled Lemon-Herb Chicken with Pink Salt – ~190 kcal
- **Dessert:** Pink Salt Chocolate Avocado Mousse – ~180 kcal

Total Daily Calories: ~980 kcal

Day 59:

- **Breakfast:** Avocado Toast with Poached Egg and Pink Salt – ~195 kcal
- **Snack:** Almond Flour Muffins with Pink Salt and Dark Chocolate Chips – ~200 kcal
- **Lunch:** Kale and Cranberry Salad with Lemon-Pink Salt Dressing – ~200 kcal

- **Snack:** Steamed Edamame with Crushed Pink Salt – ~120 kcal
- **Dinner:** Baked Salmon with Garlic, Dill, and Pink Salt – ~195 kcal
- **Dessert:** Banana Ice Cream with Pink Salt Swirl – ~120 kcal

Total Daily Calories: ~1,030 kcal

Day 60:
- **Breakfast:** Scrambled Eggs with Spinach and Pink Salt – ~170 kcal
- **Snack:** Sea Salt Caramel Energy Balls with Dates and Pink Salt – ~95 kcal
- **Lunch:** Quinoa-Stuffed Bell Peppers with Pink Salt – ~170 kcal
- **Snack:** Hummus with Olive Oil and Pink Salt Topping – ~160 kcal
- **Dinner:** Stir-Fried Tofu with Vegetables and Pink Salt Soy Glaze – ~180 kcal
- **Dessert:** Oatmeal Cookies with Pink Salt Flakes – ~95 kcal

Total Daily Calories: ~870 kcal

ABOUT THE AUTHOR

Dr. Elena Hartwell is a certified nutritionist and registered dietitian with over 15 years of experience in holistic wellness and metabolic health. After earning her PhD in Nutritional Science from the University of California, Berkeley, she dedicated her career to helping individuals transform their relationship with food through natural, evidence-based strategies.

Dr. Hartwell specializes in detoxification, anti-inflammatory diets, and sustainable weight management. Her work integrates scientific research with ancient nutritional wisdom, focusing on the therapeutic power of minerals like Himalayan pink salt and daily rituals that support long-term health.

She has consulted for wellness clinics worldwide and has been featured in several health magazines for her practical and empowering approach to diet and lifestyle. The Pink Salt Weight Loss Trick Plan reflects her passion for making wellness accessible and deeply personal for every reader.

Made in United States
Cleveland, OH
05 June 2025